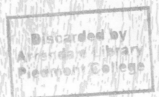

New Perspectives on Teaching and Learning

Warren Bryan Martin, *Editor*

NEW DIRECTIONS FOR TEACHING AND LEARNING
KENNETH E. EBLE and JOHN F. NOONAN, *Editors-in-Chief*

Number 7, September 1981

Paperback sourcebooks in
The Jossey-Bass Higher Education Series

Jossey-Bass Inc., Publishers
San Francisco • Washington • London

New Perspectives on Teaching and Learning
Number 7, September 1981
    Warren Bryan Martin, *Editor*

New Directions for Teaching and Learning Series
Kenneth E. Eble and John F. Noonan, *Editors-in-Chief*

New Directions for Teaching and Learning is published quarterly
by Jossey-Bass Inc., Publishers. Subscriptions, single-issue
orders, change of address notices, undelivered copies, and other
correspondence should be sent to *New Directions* Subscriptions,
Jossey-Bass Inc., Publishers, 433 California Street, San Francisco,
California 94104.

Editorial correspondence should be sent to the Editors-in-Chief,
Kenneth E. Eble or John F. Noonan, Center for Improving
Teaching Effectiveness, Virginia Commonwealth University,
Richmond, Virginia 23284.

Library of Congress Catalogue Card Number LC 80-84305
International Standard Serial Number ISSN 0271-0633
International Standard Book Number ISBN 87589-868-8

Cover art by Willi Baum
Manufactured in the United States of America

7 / 2 /82 Beehove Typ 7.95

Ordering Information

The paperback sourcebooks listed below are published quarterly and can be ordered either by subscription or single-copy.

Subscriptions cost $30.00 per year for institutions, agencies, and libraries. Individuals can subscribe at the special rate of $18.00 per year *if payment is by personal check.* (Note that the full rate of $30.00 applies if payment is by institutional check, even if the subscription is designated for an individual.) Standing orders are accepted.

Single copies are available at $6.95 when payment accompanies order, and *all single-copy orders under $25.00 must include payment.* (California, Washington, D.C., New Jersey, and New York residents please include appropriate sales tax.) For billed orders, cost per copy is $6.95 plus postage and handling. (Prices subject to change without notice.)

To ensure correct and prompt delivery, all orders must give either the *name of an individual* or an *official purchase order number.* Please submit your order as follows:

Subscriptions: specify series and subscription year.
Single Copies: specify sourcebook code and issue number (such as, IR8).

Mail orders for United States and Possessions, Latin America, Canada, Japan, Australia, and New Zealand to:
Jossey-Bass Inc., Publishers
433 California Street
San Francisco, California 94104

Mail orders for all other parts of the world to:
Jossey-Bass Limited
28 Banner Street
London EC1Y 8QE

New Directions for Teaching and Learning Series
Kenneth E. Eble and John F. Noonan, *Editors-in-Chief*

Contents

Section 2: Through Teaching, the Students Learn

Learning is the end to which teaching is a means, especially the learning done by students, yet good teaching also contributes to student learning. What the students learn when the teacher is effective are the lessons of life, as well as the materials of the course of study.

Section 3: Through Teaching, Learning to Handle Controversial Issues

Teaching and learning in America today cannot be "balanced" without making reference to political, social, and moral dimensions of contemporary life. Directly or indirectly, within the institutions of higher education or outside in the institutions of the society, it is invariably true that racism and sexism, political extremism and class distinctions, power plays and human abuses affect the lives of students and teachers, even as these social forces affect the interaction of students and teachers in the classroom.

Editor's Notes

In every person's life, and in the life of every institution, there are "moments" or incidents that may be said to typify the values and behavior of that life. Something happens with sufficient frequency to become characteristic. Or something unexpected and special occurs that, because of what it is and the way it is handled, proves to be unforgettable and influential.

The college and university teachers whose contributions provide most of the substance of this book have been willing to share with the reader various moments or incidents out of their professional lives—the little thing that looms large, the incident of the day that becomes the event of the year, the experience large or small that proves to have layers of meaning for the individual teacher and the institution of teaching and learning.

In this sourcebook, teachers themselves are talking about teaching and learning—not theoreticians or administrators, but teachers. They are talking not about financial problems or collective bargaining or the need for better facilities but discussing teaching from their own experiences, as well as from the viewpoints of their students.

We have here the teachers' reports of successes and failures. These colleagues do not present themselves as models but rather as examples. They give the reader ideas and techniques that will help other faculty members and graduate students improve their own teaching and learning. Along the way, these teachers help the reader to understand not only how important good teaching is for true learning but also how much there is to learn through teaching.

The contributors are faculty members in colleges and universities large and small in all parts of the United States. There are younger persons and older ones, with perhaps two thirds under forty-five years of age. There are women and men, about evenly represented. Three contributors are from racial minorities. As for the subject matter specializations, approximately 50 percent of the contributors are in the various disciplines of the humanities, with another 35 percent in the social and behavioral sciences, and the remaining 15 percent in the natural or physical sciences plus mathematics.

Nearly all of the teachers who share moments of their teaching experience, moments that reveal the possibilities for learning through teaching, are members of the Danforth Foundation's Graduate

1

Fellowship Program. They have held Kent fellowships, Danforth fellowships, or Graduate Fellowships for Women. Three contributors are members of the Danforth Associate Program. Two of the contributors were in graduate school at the time their statements were written, but many others tied at least one incident to their graduate experience.

The statements presented here, with two exceptions, were written in response to an invitation to these persons, and over two hundred others, to a conference on teaching and learning where emphasis would be on case studies, on actual experiences of importance to the professional lives of persons in attendance at that conference.

Respondents to the invitation were asked to prepare three short reports on positive or negative incidents in their teaching careers and, additionally, one longer and more detailed statement that would elaborate a theme or issue that they were willing to share and about which they would be glad to receive the comments of colleagues.

The statements as originally prepared were not for publication but were intended for personal discussion among trusted colleagues. Thus, even as presented here, these statements have an informal, anecdotal, personal, candid character. They have not been lightly edited; they are not in polished prose style; they were not written for literary effect.

It should also be noted that the organizers of the projected conference gave specific instructions. The Fellows were to provide a description of a personal or professional experience in each of the following areas: (1) a teaching experience that was a success; (2) a teaching experience that was a failure; (3) a learning experience that was a success; (4) a learning experience that was a failure. It was, therefore, not only from seventy-eight contributors that the statements contained in this book were selected but from four statements provided by each contributor.

The reader should remember the spirit in which the statements were solicited and supplied. One of the conference planners, and a contributor, put it this way:

> A non-competitive situation, a conference of fellows who were accustomed to meeting and discussing issues free of the hopes and fears that one's own department, institution, or specific disciplinary professional society inspires; there was nothing to lose by candor—a free situation of mutual trust.

The planning committee for the conference hoped to receive as many as two hundred statements in response to the invitation and, from that number, to choose one hundred contributors for participation in the conference. In fact, during the allotted time, seventy-eight statements were received. And from that number, thirty-eight have been selected for inclusion here.

Because of the comparatively low rate of response, and because of scheduling and financial complications, the conference was cancelled. But the statements remained. They were so rich in content, so potentially useful to college teachers that, with the permission of the authors, this collection has been put together and is here presented for the benefit of teachers across the nation.

These "teaching fellows"—fellows who are in full-time teaching—are by definition committed to give special attention to the profession of teaching, that is, they were selected as fellows through an extensive national competition that put emphasis on dedication to teaching. They are not necessarily more skilled at teaching, having had no more special training in the techniques or the art of teaching than other students in prestigious graduate schools. But, given their personal orientation and their success in the Danforth competition, it is fair to conclude that these teachers are aware of the importance of teaching, have been reflective and self-critical about their own professional lives, and have contributions to make in this ongoing discussion about teaching and learning or, as we put it, learning through teaching.

As a means of enriching the exchange of opinion that is likely to occur after a reader and his or her colleagues have completed individual sections of this book, three outstanding college teachers have written their own comments on one or another of the several clusters of reported moments and incidents. Their reactions, commendations, and criticism are found at the end of each section.

The statements of the thirty-eight contributors are grouped within sections that have separate emphases. In the first section the emphasis of the statements is that through teaching, the teacher learns— learns about personal values as well as about his or her professional orientation, learns about the extent to which the teaching techniques used are consistent with the teacher's educational philosophy and the purposes of the classroom as compared with being merely attention-getting devices. The second section features statements that show that through the teaching of teachers the student learns—learns about the development of personal character as well as about particular course content, learns to be an active participant in teaching and learning rather than a passive observer or an inert receptacle. The third section contains statements on specific problems and themes, usually quite particular issues that confront every teacher—plagiarism, racial tension in the classroom, and notions about teaching as a profession and about professionalism.

All in all, when the content of the several sections is drawn together, the reader will have confirmation that there is, even today, such a thing as learning through teaching.

Thanks to the three teacher-scholars—Elbow, Sheridan, McAloon—whose contributions provide special connective links of thought in what might otherwise be disparate statements, despite the efforts of the editor to emphasize interconnectedness.

Special thanks to Kenneth Eble, editor-in-chief of this source-book series, and to Evelyn Mercer, production manager. Their patience with the editor was exceeded only by their skill in handling materials submitted to them in a variety of formats and writing styles. Without them we would not have been able to conclude that between the differences and the unity there is no essential conflict.

Warren Bryan Martin
Editor

Warren Bryan Martin is scholar-in-residence at the Carnegie Foundation for the Advancement of Teaching, Washington, D. C. He has been vice-president of the Danforth Foundation, and has taught at three colleges and two universities.

Section 1:
Through Teaching, the Teachers Learn

*In this section, several teachers share critical
moments in their experience, which demonstrate
that teachers learn by teaching.*

Introduction

Warren Bryan Martin

Those in the profession of teaching know that the best way to learn is to
teach. True enough. But teaching is not only a wonderful way to learn
the subject matter of a discipline or the content of courses taught, it is
also a good way for the teacher to learn about what works when one is
transmitting information or explaining concepts or generating thought
and an exchange of views. Even more, teaching is a good way for a
teacher to learn about him- or herself—about personal and professional
motivations and intentions; about individual educational philosophy
and perspectives on human nature, social organization, and inter-
personal relationships; about institutional effects on individual
development.

The benefits are not only for the teacher, who through teaching
learns about teaching and about what makes him tick, the benefits are
also for the observer. As we read these reports, these moments, these
critical incidents, we learn that teaching is never mere teaching and that
finally in some measure every teacher is a model as well as a sculptor.

In the following reports of moments the authors describe key
incidents in teaching. In one a student fires a hard question: "But what
is the life of virtue? What is it *really?*" And then a friend of the teacher
reminds him that to answer the student's question may mean that the
teacher is teaching himself. In another instance, a faculty member

W. Martin (Ed.). *New Directions for Teaching and Learning: New Perspectives on Teaching and Learning,* no. 7.
San Francisco: Jossey-Bass, September 1981

became reflective and concerned by the way he dealt with an odious political ideology—and the responses to his effort. Another teacher describes how he coped with student challenges to one of the organizing principles of his course. In another report a faculty colleague recounts how he sought to be fair to others and their views while remaining definite about his own.

In the course of teaching, the teacher learns not only to review his or her personal values and social orientation, or how to deal with the basic concerns of others while carrying through with the task at hand, but the teacher also learns various techniques in teaching or ways of organizing and presenting course materials. These should be consistent with his or her own purposes while, at the same time, they should be able to catch the students' attention and enlist them in the work of teaching and learning.

Near the end of this section, there are several reports that show reactions to methods. One teacher is pleased with the success that attends the use of his personal experience as a teaching methodology, while a second teacher is compelled to reconsider his teaching style because of students' reactions to it. These two incidents, and the others, confirm a point made by Philip Rieff (1972, p. 10), a professor at the University of Pennsylvania: "I am a reteacher. The one student who takes my course again and again is myself. That course is never the same; when it becomes the same, I hope that I shall know enough to stop teaching."

*The student fires a hard question, and the teacher finds out
that in answering that question he is teaching himself.*

What Is the Life of Virtue?

James C. Edwards

This incident took place three years ago at a meeting of the Soup
Group, a small conversation club (three faculty members and
spouses, and about fifteen students) that meets weekly during term.
Someone brings a thesis, someone else prepares soup, bread, and
fruit, and we talk and eat for an hour and a half. The thesis for that
night had to do with the relationship between private morality and
institutional responsibility. I believe the discussion started when
someone deplored the use of food as a lever in international relations.
At that time, there was a great deal of concern on our campus about
world hunger, and several in our group were involved in fasts, money
raising for Oxfam, and the like; so there was almost universal
agreement that, in a world with continuing famine, food was a morally
improper bargaining chip for a nation to use. Almost universal, for
one student, John, suggested that such a judgment was itself misplaced.
There is no room, he argued, for private moral scruples in international relations. In the world of *Realpolitik*, moral considerations
simply do not apply; they are logically out of place. And this is not
unique to the international arena: at any point that one person begins
to act for another, at any point that one begins to function institution-
ally, moral considerations become otiose. Morality, John argued, has

W. Martin (Ed.). *New Directions for Teaching and Learning: New Perspectives on Teaching and Learning,* no. 7.
San Francisco: Jossey-Bass, September 1981

10

to do with individuals relating as individuals to other individuals; it is out of place in the corporate sphere.

The discussion had been going on for some time before I ventured in. In my introductory philosophy class, I had just then been reading some Plato, portraying Socrates as the paradigmatic philosopher, and leading up to his vision of the republic, a state governed by a public and reasoned conception of justice. I wanted to use Plato's account as an object of comparison, to juxtapose his conception of the state as an essentially ethical institution to the amoral conception John maintained. In the course of deploying some of the Socratic/Platonic machinery, I casually used the phrase, "the life of virtue." I said something like, "For Socrates, John, the life of virtue is virtue politically exercised. The life of virtue is marked as a mode of participation within the common life, the life of the polis, and there can be no separation of my life as a particular individual from my life as a citizen, exercising certain corporate responsibilities."

The discussion moved on, with no real focus, and soon it was time to go. But as people were moving off, John fixed me with a stare and said, "But what *is* the life of virtue?" I stumbled out some remarks on the Socratic/Platonic conception, playing the teacher, dispensing information. But he did not want that: "No, not what was Socrates's conception, but what *is* the life of virtue? What is it *really?*"

Now I was embarrassed by the question, or, rather, by my inability to know what to do with it. Here I had glibly trotted out a phrase—"the life of virtue"—trading on its power and its deep hold on our hopes, and yet I could not deliver its meaning to this man. I could say to him what great thinkers had taken the phrase to encompass, but he wanted the truth, not historical recapitulation. He was himself quite fundamentally perplexed by the scruples of his conscience confronted with (what he perceived to be) the demands of citizenship, and the way out of his quandary was apparently given in "the life of virtue." If he could just know what that meant, then he could know how to live. And that's what he wanted from me: the knowledge most worth having.

I find it terribly hard to know what to do in such situations, and I do not find those situations at all uncommon. Young people want to know what human excellence is; they are in the process of making fundamental decisions that turn on knowing that. They sense the inescapability of the question; they know they cannot answer it confidently; so they naturally ask it of others. My question is: Should I try to tell them? Not, of course, that I know the answer, but I have made my commitments, right enough, as have we all. Should I freely share these commitments, along with the doubts that accompany them, or should I sidestep into "objectivity"?

A friend of mine recently said (rather proudly, I believe) that the main change in his teaching over his first decade has been that now he mostly teaches himself, not the texts. I had to repress a shudder. I know what he means, though. By teaching certain things one puts oneself in the way of becoming an authority. If one speaks about "the life of virtue," one is sooner or later— probably sooner— going to get asked what that is. Confronted with the question, one way is just to refuse to answer, perhaps slipping back into the recapitulation of others' answers or feigning Socratic ignorance and irony. Another way is just to answer it, thus running the risks of fatuousness and preaching without authority. Is either of these ways acceptable? Is there a third way? This goes to the heart of what it is to be a teacher: Is it just to be a dispenser of information and technique, or is it also to be engaged? Should one conceive of teaching as "objectively" as possible, trying to cut out one's own commitments, or should one accede to the students' hunger for "subjectivity" in their teachers? Does one stick to teaching the texts, or does one admit to oneself that, as my friend has it, "one is always teaching oneself"?

James C. Edwards is an associate professor in the Department of Philosophy, Furman University, Greenville, South Carolina.

Sometimes it is a demand from a student, not a request or a question, that forces the teacher to think about her most fundamental purposes and make controverisal decisions that she hopes will benefit that student.

You've Got to Tell Me What's Right

Sharon E. Sutton

Several years ago I was teaching architectural design to a class of first-year students. Design is taught in a studio in which the students work while the teacher (known as the critic) visits each desk commenting on the progress of the work. This particular class was quite large. The average student was about twenty-four years old, and many of the students had other degrees or work experience.

From the very beginning one student stood out. He was quite thin and pale-looking with watery and strained eyes. His face was tense. When I sat next to him, I would see that his fingernails were dirty and that there were cuts on his hands. Perhaps he did some sort of hard labor. Maybe he should be in night school—he looked pretty worn out.

The first time I sat down at his desk, he neatly spread out about five different approaches to the problem. I was pleased to see so much work. I went over each approach saying what was good and bad and how it might be developed in a more exciting way. I complimented him on his multiple approach, but I could see toward the end of the session that he was not so pleased. I thought it best to leave him alone to work things out. I left feeling puzzled by this strange creature.

Every class this student continued to bring in an incredible number of solutions and approaches to the problem. I proceeded to

W. Martin (Ed.). *New Directions for Teaching and Learning: New Perspectives on Teaching and Learning*, no. 7. San Francisco: Jossey-Bass, September 1981

evaluate all of them, while he proceeded to become increasingly disturbed. I began to sense outright anger.

Soon there was a major review of the assignment. This student presented an elaboration of one of his many ideas. I no longer remember his solution, but I do remember that it was not outstandingly good. In my typical fashion, I therefore continued to point out what was good and what was bad and to say how it could all be improved. By this time I could definitely feel anger seething from this student.

When I arrived at the next class session, I noticed that he had taken a seat in the rear of the classroom, which, as I said, was quite overcrowded. He had also moved the last two rows of desks close to the wall so that he was virtually barricaded in the rear of the room. Because I was giving out a new assignment, everyone else was gathered in the front of the room.

The rest of the class discussed the next assignment while this student remained immobile, looking at his desk. When everyone else started to work, two choices ran through my mind—reach out to him or ignore him? Reach out to him. I climbed over the desks and demanded to know what was going on. Out blurted, "This is my only chance. I've *got* to do good. You've *got* to tell me what's right. Every week I show you my ideas, and you never say what's right. I don't have time to mess around with 'maybe this could be. . . .' I can't afford to mess up." A rather heated discussion followed in which I tried to explain the difference between ideas and answers, and he tried to explain his urgency to succeed. At some point it occurred to me that "succeed" only meant passing to him. With the rest of the class listening in disbelief, I thumped my index finger on the desk and said, "Today, right now, I am giving you your grade for the semester. That grade is to be an "A." Now I want you to begin to learn to think. Are you ready to start?"

I suppose such an impulse could have led to disaster. In a less mature classroom or with a less serious student, all discipline could have been lost. I was not sure about the class as a whole, but the remembrance of this boy with bloody hands and tired eyes repeatedly showing me so many different solutions made me take a chance. And he was worth that chance. After that screaming match—and we were screaming—this student soon became the most outstanding class participant. Not only did his own work show struggle and improvement, but he openly participated in other students' work, an essential part of learning the design process.

What was most gratifying for me was the realization that, although I had challenged this student to learn to think, he already had a highly developed and unique thought process that was being inhibited by the fear of failure. Once he was relieved of the symbol of failure, the grade, he began to explore his thoughts, to take chances on his ideas, to change directions, and to be truly creative.

Sharon E. Sutton is an architect and teaches at the Graduate School and University Center, City University of New York.

A faculty member becomes reflective and concerned about the way he dealt with an odious political ideology.

Striving for Balance Concerning an Unbalanced Ideology

Patrick J. Kelly

I will take the liberty of writing about an event in my teaching and of discussing a "thing I try to do" in one specific situation at least. It combines a learning experience I once had and the way I tried to communicate its insight recently to a class of adult students, about a third of who were Jewish.

I am a German historian and the course was on World War II in Europe. One of the things I always had trouble understanding in graduate school was that the Nazis were sincere in their hatred for the Jews. I could see why they might use the Jews as scapegoats to gain political or economic advantages, but physical annihilation was not necessary and was in fact against the Nazis' own interests because they were desperately short of labor during the war.

One day several years ago, my wife dragged me to see the movie version of *Cabaret*. There was a scene in it I will never forget. In 1932 the heroine and her friends stop by a beer garden. The other Germans there, victims of a brutal depression, are silent and sullen, simply staring at their drinks or out into space. Suddenly a handsome young man courageously stands up and begins to sing a lovely song, over and over again. At first, people ignore him, then begin to sneak furtive

W. Martin (Ed.). *New Directions for Teaching and Learning: New Perspectives on Teaching and Learning*, no. 7. San Francisco: Jossey-Bass, September 1981

glances at him, then begin to hum the song, then join in until finally an enormous crescendo of joy, love, and comradeship wells up. At the end, the camera pans back from the boy's face to show he wears a swastika armband.

Though politically I am a socialist, I could not help but be moved by the hope this boy created in a despondent people. Suddenly I understood that in a perverse sort of way, Nazism was an ideology of love, comfort, and hope for those who were insiders, and that the outsiders (foreigners, Jews) were thought to be the cause of Germany's miseries.

We are so used to rightful condemnations of the horrors the Nazis wrought that it is very difficult to convey to good, decent, middle-class Americans, some of them Jewish, how good, decent, middle-class Germans could follow and even idolize a Hitler who we are taught was a grotesque combination of maniac and buffoon.

I tried to communicate to this class a picture of Nazism as seen by Germans who were like themselves— how what appears to outsiders as hatred and prejudice can appear to insiders as love and fellowship. At first they resisted, but I was, after a while, quite successful in seducing some of them into seeing it from the inside. In several cases, alas I was too successful, and I am afraid, despite my later condemnations, that some wound up with a better impression of Nazism than it deserves.

This situation and others like it pose a testy pedagogical and moral problem. On one hand, teachers should present all points of view sympathetically, from the inside, even as loathsome an idea as Nazism. Without this approach, history, at least, becomes incomprehensible. On the other hand, we have the responsibility to get students to think critically about all points of view.

Did I go too far by demonstrating that the Nazis solved the unemployment of the depression, and restored a form of dignity and self-respect to the Germans? I firmly believe that if an American president promised to cure inflation and unemployment and to make the United States "number one" again (whatever that means) and above all delivered on those promises, most decent, middle-class Americans would rejoice if the only price were, for example, to deport all the Puerto Ricans. How do we teach people to see the "Nazi" in themselves? Is it worth the risk of making some of them "Nazis"?

In this particular situation, is it worth the pain, especially to the Jewish students, to help them understand why the Nazis hated the Jews and most Germans were sullenly indifferent or mutteringly hostile toward them? So far my answers to these questions have been anxious yesses. Sometimes I wonder whether they are the right answers, or whether I could get the same learning effect in a more sensitive or intelligent way. Was this learning experience a success or a failure?

Patrick J. Kelly is a member of the Department of History, Adelphi University, Garden City, New York.

*A faculty member realizes that the influence of family and
church may be more powerful than that of a college-level course.*

Confronting Fundamentalist
Beliefs in a Biology Course

Judith H. Sumner

Before this past year, I had never lived nor taught in the South.
Probably I had all of the stereotypes and prejudices in my mind that
Northerners have about Southerners, but I must admit that I had not
even considered the persuasive influence of fundamentalist religion. I
had signed on to teach at a small Presbyterian college, but anticipated
no problems. After all, during my hiring seminar I had spoken on the
principles of Darwinian evolution as they apply to the evolution of
plant species on islands. The talk had been well received. I foresaw no
conflict between the concepts of religion and the teaching of the
principles of evolution.

As a biologist, I stress evolution as a unifying theory. In every
course, whether at the cellular or organismic level, I attempt to
integrate putative evolutionary trends into the overall picture. I
interpret evolution as a means by which to resolve a huge number of
disparate facts and a wealth of qualitative and quantitative information
into a logical sequence. As a scientist, I am oriented toward problem
solving. The accumulation of facts is work; the organization and
interpretation of these facts is delight. This is the philosophy with
which I approach the study of biology.

W. Martin (Ed.). *New Directions for Teaching and Learning: New Perspectives on Teaching and Learning,* no. 7.
San Francisco: Jossey-Bass, September 1981

It was several months before I realized that David, a junior biology major who had taken three of my courses, was consistently unwilling to engage in any dialogue that had even remotely evolutionary overtones. When I assigned two chapters in Darwin's *Origin of Species,* he declined to read them. Subsequently he told me that he considered Darwin to be a tool of Satan and that I also had the devil at work inside of me. I was taken aback by this.

A day or two later, I discovered that two other students in the class agreed with David. All three were upperclassmen, two majoring in biology and one in chemistry. For months, actually years, not one of them had made his views known. At the time, I found this very disturbing. How could these students dutifully copy down and recite back on exams information that they found religiously repugnant, without even once mentioning the conflict in their minds? Why had they never even hinted at their beliefs? Was I that intimidating? I did not think so.

There were many other questions that I found difficult to resolve. How could these young people, all basically sound students, be so willing to reject such a unifying principle, such a biologically appealing theory? I thought that surely we must be failing in our teaching of the methods and philosophy of science.

A few days after this revelation, David returned to my office with an antievolution religious tract, written (curiously) in the format of a comic book. The story line itself was fairly sophisticated, and I can only assume that it was written to appeal to adults perceived as ignorant by the religious press in California who produced it. He had made a special trip to a local Christian bookstore to pick it up. He asked that I read it, commenting that it would help me in the recognition of the truth. Out of curiosity (and some degree of perversity), I accepted the comic book and read it at home that evening. I listed all of the supposed scientific facts used to negate the theory of evolution and the process of natural selection. Several were misstatements or information taken out of context. I noted a number of comments on the sheet. Naively, I thought that I could help these students see the light. The next day, David came in to solicit my opinion. I pointed out to him some of the specious reasoning and inaccurate information being used by the author of the comic book to counter evolutionary theory. Perhaps his most memorable argument was one centering on the disappearance of the skeletal remains of Peking Man. The gist of the argument was that since the bones "mysteriously disappeared," this putative hominid was actually a hoax. The bones did actually disappear when they were being shipped by rail; likely they were just lost, if Occam's Razor applies to daily living. David could see no problem with any of the material that I criticized. He remained steadfast. As a teacher of biology, I felt like a washout. Later that evening, I decided that I was a fool ever to become involved in this dialogue. The influence of family and church was obviously much more powerful than that of a college-level course.

I had answers to none of my questions, and I still do not. After the end of classes, David left me another small pamphlet with an antievolutionary message. Earlier, at about the time of final exams, we were talking about graduate school, and I felt obliged to tell him that his steadfast rejection of evolutionary theory could be a serious liability in a graduate program in biology. His only answer was that he would continue to present me with additional literature, with the eventual goal of turning my beliefs from evolution to special creation. I really could not respond to this.

While this incident has had no direct effect on my teaching, it has taught me a tremendous amount about the strength of religious convictions and the impact of emotional arguments on the human mind. It seems to me that as college teachers we often dictate factual material, simultaneously assuming that our students believe everything that we say. At first, it was alarming to me that this is not the case, especially in the case of upperclassmen involved with their major discipline. In retrospect, I have had to realize that many other people and factors influence the perceptions of our students.

Judith H. Sumner is a teacher in the Department of Biology, Maryville College, Maryville, Tennessee.

A student learns that contradictory positions can be argued convincingly without undercutting a teacher's credibility.

Respecting and Criticizing Conflicting Viewpoints

Jerry A. Irish

It was a course that examined major figures in Western philosophy and theology. The first several weeks were spent on Plato, and I was absolutely convinced that there could be no more comprehensive world view. Nor could I imagine any significant criticism of Plato's work. It was also apparent to me, as it was to the other students in the course, that the professor shared Plato's views. Indeed, the word was around that in graduate school he had received high praise from a renowned Plato scholar.

I was taken by surprise when we turned to the study of Aristotle and this same professor began to point out weaknesses in Plato's philosophy. The better our grasp of Aristotle, the more questions we had for Plato. At the completion of the section on Aristotle, we had all come to the realization that this was the fully adequate system, free of the shortcomings we now recognized in Plato. The oral tradition surrounding our professor had also been modified. We marveled at this grasp of Plato, given his own clear preference for Aristotle.

It was not long, of course, before Aristotle's position began to falter in comparison with subsequent world views. Indeed, the pattern

W. Martin (Ed.). *New Directions for Teaching and Learning: New Perspectives on Teaching and Learning,* no. 7. San Francisco: Jossey-Bass, September 1981

of thoroughly favorable presentation followed by criticism in light of the next philosopher or theologian continued throughout the course. As our own critical capacities sharpened, we began to anticipate problems in a particular position before they were pointed out to us. But the professor never wavered from the pattern he had established; he never challenged a scheme before he had presented it in the most favorable light.

As the course progressed, the strengths and weaknesses of earlier figures took on different meaning. We began to see that there were trade-offs in any system of thought, and these trade-offs were impossible to assess apart from our own experience. And now we were not at all sure what the professor's own position was. Perhaps he favored Plato after all. One thing was clear—he had a tremendous respect for reason rigorously employed in the exploration of the human condition. In no course since then have I learned so much philosophy and theology or so much about the process of humanistic thought and the value of entertaining alternative visions of the world.

The course in question was demanding and fascinating; I would not have missed a lecture or skipped a reading for anything. While I sensed the value of what was going on at the time, it has only been in recent years that I have come to appreciate the teaching of such a course. After some reflection, I am not at all sure how the professor presented the material as he did without ever giving us the impression that we were playing a game. We never caught the debilitating diseases associated with relativism. We had the sense that despite particular forms of nearsightedness, each figure in the course contributed not only to the history of ideas, but to our own understanding of the present. The fact that two contradictory positions could be argued convincingly did not undercut the whole enterprise. Indeed, as manifested by this professor, the enterprise became all the more interesting. There was a kind of passion involved in our study. This is especially puzzling to me now as I recall no instances in which the professor made references to his own beliefs, values, or concerns. The painstaking examination of philosophical and theological material was broken only by an occasional movie review or reference to the Civil War. Even these often humorous anecdotes turned out to be tangents rather than diversions.

Now that I am a teacher myself in a time when the pursuit of ideas has few participants, I think back on that course and ask myself "How did he do it?"

Jerry A. Irish is provost and professor of religion, Kenyon College, Gambier, Ohio.

An anecdote about the teacher's honeymoon and certain bodily functions leads to useful information about human relationships as well as about an important physiological principle.

Using the Personal (Very Personal) Anecdote

David R. Mouw

Over the past eight years, I have had the privilege (sometimes as I walk down to the auditorium, I catch myself saying, "you actually get paid for doing this") of giving about 550 lectures in general human physiology to classfuls of about 275 students, in addition to my other teaching responsibilities. When I think of these totals, I am a bit frightened at the awesome responsibility of it all, and the number of student lecture minutes I have wasted by being unclear, wrong, or inefficient or by telling "stories." Actually, upon second thought, while the stories might at first appear to be wasted time, they have, I feel, served a valuable function in this large-lecture type of teaching. Here is the rationale.

In order for an anecdote to qualify for inclusion in one of my lectures, it has to meet at least one, and usually all, of the following criteria. (1) Most importantly it must illustrate the physiological principle that I am trying to teach. (2) Listening to the anecdote should be so reinforcing (enjoyable) that the listener, awakened from stupor by the familiarity of the introduction, "that reminds me of . . .," is immediately engrossed in the story. This awakening reflex should be facilitated by the listener's past experience with such stories, and thus

W. Martin (Ed.). *New Directions for Teaching and Learning: New Perspectives on Teaching and Learning*, no. 7. San Francisco: Jossey-Bass, September 1981

my technique lends itself much better to cases in which one professor gives a long lecture, sequence, or an entire course. (3) Preferably, the story should be personal and should, in the process of its telling, reveal the professor as a person. It is quite appropriate if some of the instructor's idiosyncrasies, moral outlooks, and personal history are revealed. This greatly facilitates a student's getting to know the teacher and relating to him or her personally, which in turn makes it easier for the teacher to fill his or her function as a role model. (4) The anecdote should be one that the students can relate to personally, a situation like one in which they have found themselves. This is particularly easy in my field of study because human physiology is so relevant in each individual's daily life. (5) It is nice if the anecdote is funny or has funny aspects, although this is not essential. This of course relates to the reinforcing properties mentioned in number two. Often the anecdote may be a sort of joke.

The best way to fully describe what I am trying to do with anecdotes is to tell one that I feel meets most of the above criteria. I am afraid that writing it down will not be quite like telling it orally, and I fear that much of the success of such stories and their funny aspects has to do with the students getting to know me. I have so many stories, I hardly know which one to pick, but here goes anyway.

Physiological principle: Urine is essentially composed not of waste products* (the kidney is not a garbage disposal unit), but rather of water and salts such as KCl and $NaCl$) which are present in the body in excess. This is the "balance concept": since salts are neither synthesized nor catabolized, intake of $Na+$ in food and drink in an adult who has reached stable body size equals output in feces, sweat (minor and poorly controlled), and urine. The only one of these three variables (oral intake, fecal/sweat output, renal output) that is regulated physiologically is renal output. One of the most interesting, perplexing, and clinically important questions the renal physiologist faces is how the kidney "knows" just the right amount of $Na+$ to excrete so that over a wide range of $Na+$ intakes, the body content of $Na+$ remains virtually constant. That is, in physiological terms, what are the control signals sent to the kidney? When these mechanisms fail, $Na+$ retention can result, and high blood pressure with eventual heart failure is often

---

* Urine contains significant amounts of urea, a true waste product of protein catabolism, but it is not a toxin and zero output for several days is harmless, as is the ingestion of urea (it is fed to cattle). Over the long run (weeks), failure of urea excretion is part of the syndrome of uremic poisoning (which is fatal), but the point here is that in the course of normal day-to-day functioning, by far the most important role of the kidneys is regulation of the correct balance of salt and water in the body.

the sequel. So, urine is essentially composed of very "good" ingredients—chemicals that are essential in the body–which happen to be in temporary excess, and the kidney, in its regulatory role, excretes them. Thus, the ingestion of urine would be completely harmless and would simply mean that, as a result of appropriate signals to the kidney, a little more would be excreted in the urine over the next twenty-four hours.

That reminds me of an experience I had on my honeymoon. Karen and I had decided to take a canoe trip for one week in a wilderness area of Michigan's upper peninsula on the Manistique River in the Seney Wildlife Refuge. As it turned out, we had a super time, but not until we solved several perplexing problems. One of them had to do with the mosquitos, which were out in hordes every evening. It was so bad (thank goodness we had a tent with a bottom and a zippered mosquito netting inside the front door), that we developed the technique of dashing around the woods to ditch the mosquitos, then ducking under the front netting, and quickly zippering it shut so that the mosquitos would not follow us in. So we did not have the mosquitos in the tent, which, with all the available skin surface area, would have been a serious problem all in itself. However, there was still a difficult situation to be faced: emptying your bladder after you were settled in the tent meant you had to get completely dressed, expose yourself to the mosquitos while voiding outside (and let mosquitos in as you left), then do the dash in the woods, before struggling back into the tent. The fact that our bladders always seemed to get full before we were ready to leave the tent probably was caused by the early hour at which we went to bed and the long time we seemed to enjoy spending there.*
It was obvious that we needed some sort of "indoor" toilet—a container of some type. Simply using the container in front of each other within the confines of the small tent would demand an element of frankness and openness, but we thought we could deal with that. The trouble was, we could not come up with a container. In the interest of light packing,

---

*Later in the course, while discussing the physiology of human sexual response, and the Masters and Johnson work, I feel it is important to put that physiology in the context of human relationships. I do not hesitate to imply that Karen and I went into those long tent nights as virgins (which happens to have been the case). I do not in the slightest sense do this in a self-righteous manner, but only in the sense of revealing a bit of my own personal history, showing the changing times, helping the virgins in the class to feel a little more at ease (the pressure is actually on them), and by way of saying that in my own humble opinion, sex outside the context of personal relationship and commitment, is less likely to be fully as satisfying—an opinion incidentally heartily reinforced by one of the later Masters and Johnson books, *The Pleasure Bond.*

I had not taken canned goods, and we had no milk containers. The only thing we could come up with was our coffee pot. Knowing that there was nothing harmful in urine, except maybe a few bacteria from the urethral orifice that would be easily killed by boiling, I convinced Karen that this was obviously our toilet. That was the solution we arrived at and it worked very well. Each morning, after emptying the urine, we would give it a quick rinse in the river and fill it for boiling coffee. And it was some of the best coffee I have ever had.

I fully appreciate that this type of lecture approach is not for every one, but somehow in a teacher-student relationship of which I can never fully understand the chemistry, for my low-keyed I'm-just-doing-the-best-I-can style, it seems to have worked reasonably well. Most students greatly appreciate what they take as "honest openness" (which I believe it is), and very few students have ever taken offense. In one of the nicest personal comments I have ever received at the end of the term, either orally or in the written evaluation, I had a student say to me "if you were the rabbi in charge, I'd come to synagogue every week." (The student has perceived correctly that some parts of my science lectures bear a striking resemblance to sermons.)

In 1974 I had the good fortune to be honored with what the University of Michigan calls the distinguished service award for excellence in teaching. The citation from the University of Michigan President Robin Flemming read in part: "Dr. Mouw stands out for that uncommon ability to transform even a large classroom with hundreds of students into a challenging and satisfying learning experience. . . . he conveys to (the students) his own love of life and respect for living things, and his obvious interest and concern. . . ." If there is any truth in it, it may be due in no small part to the richness of experiences that I have been fortunate to have in my first thirty-seven years and the willingness to share those which are relevant to physiology in an open, frank, and easy going manner with my students. When it is all said and done, I have really enjoyed telling the stories, and I think the students enjoyed hearing them, and perhaps that is justification enough. In any case, when I talk to students a few years later, they always remember the honeymoon coffeepot, and sometimes they even remember the regulatory role of the kidney and balance concept!

David R. Mouw is an associate professor in the Department of Physiology at the University of Michigan Medical School, Ann Arbor.

A teacher ponders the positive and negative effects of
maintaining an aggressive teaching style.

Aggressive Teaching Reconsidered

Byron A. Nichols

After eleven years of teaching, I am being forced to reconsider my basic teaching style. There are moral issues involved in this reassessment as well as empirical questions about current students. What makes this reconsideration a bit ironic is that by all conventional standards my teaching has been held out as among the best at the college. The issue is really whether continuing to do the same thing will produce different results and different reactions than previously. What pains me in the reconsideration process is that I have derived deep satisfaction from what I have done, and I continue to enjoy many of the more personal side benefits.

Probably the best word to describe my style is "aggressive," both in the sense of the intellectual challenge it offers to students and in its being personally intense. I rarely lecture in class: I call on students at random for a dialogue about the material we have been reading (not questions of fact from the books but questions about an author's logic and assumptions and the relationship between his or her arguments and those of other authors in the course). I deliberately pick the best books in the field regardless of their complexity or turgidity. I never give tests; students are always required to submit analytic course material. I never grade papers knowing who wrote them, for fear that personalities will color my comments; I prefer to

W. Martin (Ed.). *New Directions for Teaching and Learning: New Perspectives on Teaching and Learning*, no. 7.
San Francisco: Jossey-Bass, September 1981

grade anonymously so that I am free to respond to arguments qua arguments. My favorite question, "So what?" constantly forces students to defend their reasoning and sharpen their arguments. I refuse to take silence as an answer, nor will I accept "I don't know" since all students know something if they have done the reading. I am convinced—and I have been ever since graduate school—that learning is never attained in a passive stance. Almost everything in my teaching is a deliberate strategy to force students into an active engagement with both the academic world and the larger environment of which they are part. Fortunately, teaching political science offers a perfect vehicle for such a strategy.

Leaving aside what I presume to be the obvious intellectual and pedagogical benefits from such a teaching strategy, this particular approach has also produced a number of unintended but deeply gratifying, personal rewards. First, I see a disproportionately large number of the college's best students. Not only do these students usually enjoy the kind of courses I teach, but they seek them out regardless of discipline; my classes therefore often contain an unusual mixture of academic backgrounds. The result is upper-level courses with some of the most stimulating, articulate, challenging students on campus—the kind who let me get away with nothing and who ask to hold class on their own if I have to be away. Second, I see a disproportionately large number of students with solid ego strength and maturity. Being bombarded constantly with questions and with essay topics that defy formulaic responses can be intimidating and threatening, and the students who enjoy the intellectual challenge also tend to be those who have self-awareness and self-confidence. This is precisely the kind of students with whom it is quickly possible to establish a personal relationship that transcends the boundary of teacher-student roles. Third, and finally, it has permitted me to maintain a lasting, human relationship with individual students that endures far beyond their graduation. A very unusual deep bond occurs among individuals for whom "good questions" matter far more than "good answers." In sum, my particular teaching style has resulted in a degree of personal satisfaction that I had not really expected and that continues to sustain me after eleven years in the classroom.

But on the negative side, there is a series of costs that make me wonder—professionally and personally—about the wisdom of continuing to be aggressive. First, very few students arrive at college with any really developed inquisitiveness. Lulled by high school curricula that equate memorization with knowledge and by the current culture of immediate gratification, most entering freshmen have no sense of what it means to "think" or of how hard thinking really is. They, therefore, tend to quickly "turn off" my kind of course, either missing the point of it completely or never enrolling to begin with. My concern is that most of these students are capable of independent, sophisticated thinking, but like anything with which they are not familiar, they need considerable practice, constant encouragement, and subtle selling. It may, indeed, be counterproductive to greet them with what amounts to total immersion.

Second, it is never fun to be "blasted" by unhappy students, whether in anonymous course evaluations, private comments to my department chairman, or—rarely—in face-to-face discussion. An aggressive instructor is often perceived as intimidating, insensitive, and even vindictive. I am not quite sure how to react when a student writes on his course evaluation, "This was probably the best course I ever took, but I hate you." Because many students really never fully understand what I am doing in my teaching or why I am doing it (despite frequent explanations and reminders on my part), they are frustrated and angered.

Third, and probably most important, my style is particularly hard on students who are shy, retiring, and lack self-confidence. Even though I am generally perceptive enough to sense when someone is panicked or frightened and will try to ease them into a discussion or essay, it is never easy to have to think out loud in front of thirty other students or to commit something on paper for official "judgment" by the instructor. These wallflowers are just as sensitive, just as eager, just as anguished, and just as craving of praise and attention as are the ego-strong and the intellectually brave. But they are easily hurt and dispirited. Instead of helping to develop their mental skills, I wind up leading them to believe that they cannot think at all. The Director of the Counselling Center once told me—only half in jest—that he never needed to look at the catalog to know when I was teaching the freshman course.

My problem now is to decide whether to change, and if so, how and how much. Part of my dilemma is moral or ethical in nature, involving questions of the principles of faculty-student relationships. Such questions include:

- Am I responsible to every student equally in my classes, or does some principle of equitability imply that I can teach to the better students?
- Am I responsible to principles and convictions I have about the importance of independent thought and well-argued

34

viewpoints, or am I responsible to students as individuals with human needs?

- Are a student's ego-defense needs a legitimate professional concern of the teacher-scholar? Why?
- Is there anything morally wrong if a student feels fear in an academic or classroom setting?
- Is there anything wrong if I wind up with smaller classes filled with many of the best students while my colleagues correspondingly have to deal with larger classes and more mediocre students?
- Is there anything wrong with being disliked by students if they succeed according to the instructor's criteria and if they appreciate their success?

But part of my dilemma is also empirical in nature, referential to the kind of student now matriculating in the best colleges in the country. It may be that students are no longer able to respond to the content of my demands or to understand the significance of independent inquiry.

Byron A. Nichols is an associate professor in the Department of Political Science at Union College, Schenectady, New York.

A dream assignment causes a teacher to worry that it may be "too good" and to consider what effect he wants to have as a teacher.

Tapping Student Interests and Concerns

Michael Schudsen

I teach in a year-long social science sequence for freshmen. Called Self, Culture, and Society, it focuses on works by Marx, Weber, Durkheim, and Freud. The second quarter concerns different symbolic systems. We read on the nature of language, on ritual, on myths, on dreams, and sometimes on science. For the study of dreams, students read large chunks of Freud's *The Interpretation of Dreams.* Some time in advance of this part of the course, I tell students to try to remember their dreams and to write them down because I will be asking them to interpret one of their own dreams, using *The Interpretation of Dreams* as a kind of manual. This assignment, both years I have tried it, has proved a centerpiece of the course

For the students, this is the one assignment almost all of them get deeply involved in. As a group, the "dream papers" are of higher quality than any other papers during the year. In part, of course, it is hard to "grade" someone's interpretation of his or her own dreams. But it seems clear to me that most of the students work with and work over the dreams, trying out interpretations and abandoning them, talking to friends about the dream and getting additional views, going back to the text and reading it with an eye to being able to use it.

W. Martin (Ed.). *New Directions for Teaching and Learning: New Perspectives on Teaching and Learning,* no. 7. San Francisco: Jossey-Bass, September 1981

Reading becomes less rote, more purposeful. The papers are very serious but also, very often, more playful than any others that the students write.

One of the problems with the assignment is that, in a way, it is too good. In teaching one spends a long time trying to affect or influence a student. Then, wondrously, one finds an exercise that deeply affects at least a few weeks of a student's life and directly shapes the student's comprehension of an important text. And yet it raises a problem of how much and what kind of effect I want to have as a teacher. Let me offer an example.

One student wrote on a dream about being assaulted and robbed on a dark street. The dream centered on an actual incident in the student's life, an incident that she had not told her mother about. In interpreting the dream, she felt that the dream showed a great deal of conflict about her decision to keep the robbery from her mother. She came to me to ask if she could have her "dream paper" returned soon because she was going home for the weekend and, after writing the paper, decided she should tell her mother. She wanted to tell her mother by showing her the paper.

As it turned out, her mother expressed little alarm at the robbery and no surprise that her daughter had not told her about it. Indeed, she said, it was quite like her to keep things to herself until she had worked through them. And she told the student how this fit patterns in her personality that had been evident in early childhood.

On the one hand, I was as delighted as could be to have stimulated some real searching in this student and in many others. The students, too, were delighted with their own skills at interpretation and their own insights into themselves. On the other hand, I wondered if I should have this much influence or this kind of influence. Some of the students overinterpreted their dreams and assigned various labels of psychopathology to themselves that were not at all warranted by what they found in the dreams. I told the students this in my comments on their papers and in some general remarks I felt called upon to make to the class as a whole. But which lesson stuck?

Where I have some doubts, then, about the assignment for the students, I have no doubt about the value of the assignment for the teacher. We ordinarily encounter students in such a thin slice of their lives, and I and, I think, many others forget what eighteen-year-olds away from home for the first time and away from the friends they grew up with are experiencing. The dreams have various themes. Among the ones that struck me are concerns about relations with parents, which frequently undergo considerable strain and change at this period; concerns about competence in school; concerns about the school itself and whether one chose the right place or should have gone to one of the other schools that offered admission; concerns about sex, drugs, and first encounters with unfamiliar social expectations; concerns about loneliness, roommates, and finding friends.

In the abstract, of course, I certainly knew that the eighty minutes twice a week during which I saw these students was not the whole of their lives. But reading their dream papers, I wanted to kick myself for not concretely keeping that in mind. What difference would it make? I do not think that I would care any less about reading Marx, Weber, Durkheim, and Freud with them, but there might be ways the caring would be better oriented to their needs. I do not know. I do know that when I asked students if I could xerox copies of their dream papers for possible use in teaching teachers and sensitizing them to the private lives of their students, most of the students eagerly assented and several volunteered their opinions that it would be an excellent thing to do.

Michael Schudsen is an associate professor in the Department of Sociology at the University of California at San Diego.

Extraneous pressures break down a teacher's "professional" presentation of complex ideas and allow his personal enthusiasm to break through.

When Determined "Muddling Through" Paid Off

Peter Manchester

As a visiting professor, I had not met any students yet and had no good idea what range of abilities or, more crucial, backgrounds would turn out for my upper-division seminar in theology. I did feel a definite need to make a good impression on my colleagues with the course since it lay smack in the middle of my own area of expertise. So I targeted a topic in which I had long experience, all the way back to my dissertation.

My ambitious syllabus was quickly subjected to serious strains, however, when the group proved to contain twenty students of great eagerness but next to no background in study of religion in general, much less in the complex issues in philosophical theology to which my topic attached. My early lectures were so far beyond their range of associations that only a couple of students were even able to ask relevant questions. As weeks wore on, I adapted with accelerating success to their level of experience, but one student in particular still seemed out of contact with the course.

She was a young woman, a foreign student, whose extreme shyness was exacerbated by the limitations of her English (which were nowhere near as severe as she felt them to be), but who had shown considerable analytical power in her first exam and was the only class

W. Martin (Ed.). *New Directions for Teaching and Learning: New Perspectives on Teaching and Learning*, no. 7. San Francisco: Jossey-Bass, September 1981

member who had plainly done all the assigned reading. Her diligence with the material seemed sure to give me the leverage to draw her out a little, to get her to participate in class discussion. But even when she would have a brief question after class, my first sketch of an answer would be enough for her and she would all but flee from any hint of a more engaged interchange. She seemed to constellate in person the continuing veil that hung between my intentions for the course and the group's actual work.

Then came the week in which a series of false bomb threats on campus reduced everyone to distraction and irritation. In my course, we were coming up on a core of crucial, difficult problems in a text by Augustine, and I had planned on preparing a masterpiece of a simplifying, organizing, and orientating lecture. But two afternoon-long evacuations of my office building had left no time to do it properly, and so I set out for the pivotal class with only rough notes and a fingers-crossed reliance on the capacity of pure presence-of-mind to be at least orderly and clear.

Before I could begin, someone appeared in the door to say that the building was being evacuated, there was another bomb threat. Grim with frustration and fury, I led us to another building—my prepared lecture now in tatters and shards, my presence-of-mind completely wrecked. Too stubborn to adjourn, I fell back on a complicated question about the nature of "will" that figured large in my own work and writing, but which I had not planned to introduce for many weeks in the course. As a sort of warhorse theme in my inventory of packaged treatments, I thought I could at least lay it out in a preliminary way that would not seem too far out of place and in any case would save the hour.

But sure enough, in my distracted frame of mind, all of the deep technical problems I had trained myself to perceive began to obtrude. I heard my presentation becoming more convoluted, watched glowers begin to appear on faces. It seemed like I was talking too fast, and on top of everything else was becoming hopelessly confused. It approached that vaguely nightmarish experience the psychologists call "deperson-alization," when it seems like you are watching and listening to yourself as though some stranger, seen from above and behind your own head. At the end of the hour, I fled the classroom with the starkest sense of failure—of imposition upon poor undergraduates, of wasted time.

The next afternoon the young foreign student appeared in my office, saying she wanted some help with the previous day's lecture. I immediately launched into an apology, berating the childishness of the bomb threats, beating my breast over the confusing presentation—until she interrupted to say that was not her problem. She had come in not to ask for help with a confused lecture, but to seek advice concerning a deeply personal decision she had never been able to parse out for herself, which she said my "wonderful lecture" had finally illuminated for her. The basic distinction I had drawn (between will as choice and will as wholeheartedness in action) had come through to her with perfect clarity, and the application of it she had seen in her life was a revelation—for me as much as her. We spent at least two hours in a remarkable and rewarding conversation.

When final exams finally came in, I discovered that no other point I had made all semester had registered with the whole class with the clarity of that afternoon's struggle with "will" in the mud of distraction, disorientation, and a foul mood. This little episode has shown me that there are still new dimensions to explore in what I early saw was one of the key facts about lecturing: What one means to say or thinks one has said and what one is actually heard to have said are very different things. In this case, I was trying as consciously as possible all semester to modulate my syllabus and presentations by the reactions and interests of the group, but I see that I was still not breaking out of the circle of my own perceptions and expectations. Too much management, not enough adventure. Only after my "professionalism" was broken down by extraneous hassle did I manage to let loose an effective dose of my basic enthusiasm for the material and to expose them to a genuinely earnest (it felt like a struggle to survive!) intellectual exertion.

Among other reflections the experience provokes, I begin to realize why my first years of teaching went so well, despite what now seems to have been the recklessness with which I then ignored class level, niceties of syllabus construction, and the like. Students respond to you best when you are actually doing something that engages you. I am considering wasting less energy on production values this coming year, spending more time on the tightrope in class. It could be that the drama of thought is more compelling than its finish.

Peter Manchester is assistant professor of religious studies at the State University of New York, Stony Brook.

Is it a teacher's business to try to develop a student's sense of responsibility as well as to get across the materials of the course?

He Was Furious

Kristin Morrison

He had arrived forty minutes late for a two-hour final exam (one long essay), and I did not extend the time for him; he had had to turn in his paper when the other students did. Later in my office, he berated me, saying I was rigid and unbending, treated them all like grade-school children, was just a school marm, not a real college professor. He claimed a good excuse; he had had unavoidable, verifiable car trouble.

This student had been quite late regularly throughout the semester, had seemed to me cavalier in his manner, perhaps "testing the limits." Other students seemed to not be bothered by the fact that I required attendance and took roll (participation was an important part of the class). Other students came to class regularly; other students managed to get to the exam on time.

One of the things I have discovered in twenty years of teaching is that students will meet deadlines that they know are firm (I have colleagues who are flooded with late papers and make-up exams; that rarely happens in my courses). But I have also found that there is a prevailing attitude that rules do not apply if you have some kind of excuse. (It can be any excuse: "My family always goes to Phoenix for vacation during this next week, so I'll be missing the exam; shall I take it before I leave or after I get back?")

W. Martin (Ed.). *New Directions for Teaching and Learning: New Perspectives on Teaching and Learning*, no. 7. San Francisco: Jossey-Bass, September 1981.

I worry about what kind of preparation for life in the "real world" this acceptance of excuses gives our students. So I tried to explain to this particular angry student that it was not his intention but his effected action that was the issue. I did not feel angry toward him, nor punitive. But I did feel uncomfortable because of his anger. I felt that all his rebellion against authority was being dumped on me (this was in the late 1960s), and that all his adolescent male resentment against mothers and women teachers was being directed against me. But maybe that was my own defensiveness, focusing on how he was "in the wrong," explaining his hang-ups, when in fact I do have some of my own regarding rigidity. Yet, to give a fuller picture, I must add that the class session itself was very "free," with an unpredictable formlessness. Most of the students in anonymous evaluations rated the course very highly, many saying it was the best course they had ever taken.

I guess what I wanted to teach this student, in addition to the actual material of the course, was a sense of responsibility for his own actions even in a world where every variable cannot be controlled. But is that any of my business? What, in fact, did he learn? All I know is that he was angry and abusive, and that I felt uncomfortable and vaguely guilty.

Kristin Morrison is an associate professor in the Department of English at Boston College, Massachusetts.

A conversation in which student, teacher, and alter ego debate the issue of teacher as performer.

Student, Teacher, Ghost

Hillel Schwartz

Student: That was a great class! I still remember that wheel of fortune.
Teacher: Well, it was a gimmick to get everyone in that large class to talk to me.
Ghost: Yes, it was a gimmick. A good teacher should not use gimmicks. Ask the student how the wheel of fortune related to the intellectual substance of your course.
Teacher: And it worked. On the first day of class, with 150 students. But how many students do you think would still be able to tell me how the wheel of fortune related to the course?
Student: I don't know. I mean, I can see how it related: grades, fame, you know, the whole Renaissance thing, and . . . clocks.
Teacher: Uh-huh.
Ghost: Uh-huh?
Student: Anyway, you really kept us interested. It was my favorite class. I only ditched it when I had a biochem exam the next day. I never knew what was going to happen next—music, slides, you dancing around or lecturing from the back of the room. . . .
Ghost: In other words, you were a performer. An entertainer. You catered to the whims of an adolescent audience.
Teacher: Yes, I was a performer, wasn't I?

W. Martin (Ed.). *New Directions for Teaching and Learning: New Perspectives on Teaching and Learning,* no. 7. San Francisco: Jossey-Bass, September 1981

Student: What? Oh yeah, I guess you were. But I really worked hard in your class—it was my hardest class. I spent more hours writing those weird papers for you than I did on all my other courses combined—except maybe for biochem.

Teacher: What did you get out of doing those papers?

Ghost: You're just a performer begging for applause.

Student: I had to think. I mean, everyone knew that you were going to read our papers, and after that first time when they saw they couldn't get away with things like they could with the TAs. . . .

Ghost: So you wanted the limelight so much that you shoved the TAs back into the shadows, right?

Teacher: Didn't the TAs help you?

Student: No, not really. Well, maybe Chris; I heard that Chris was really a good TA, but I didn't have her.

Teacher: What was wrong with your TA?

Student: I don't know, I guess being a TA is pretty hard, but my TA just didn't know very much. I mean, he was as confused as we were by some of your lectures.

Ghost: If your lectures were confusing, you must have had more style than substance. A pure performer. Such performances do not belong in universities. Remember Socrates devastating the rhetorician?

Teacher: In what way were some of my lectures confusing?

Student: Well, not exactly confusing. It's just that there was so much in your lectures, so much to think about, and one day it was armor and women's clothing, the next day the Black Death, and art, and all those dates, and. . . .

Teacher: (to ghost): There, you see.

Ghost: See what? Smorgasbord. Vaudeville. Variety shows. Who ever grasped the fundamentals of the humanities from the Minskys?

Teacher: Wait a minute. Now it seems you are arguing not only against theatricality but against popular culture.

Student: What?

Teacher: Oh, I'm sorry, excuse me, I was talking to myself. You see, I've been worrying about that humanities course. I've been wondering whether all that energy I put into the drama and excitement of it was, well, misplaced.

Ghost: Understatement.

Student: Not at all. I learned more from your class than I did from the humanities courses in the fall or winter. You know, people used to pay people to bring cassettes to lectures in those classes, so they wouldn't have to go. That never happened in your class. We still talk about your lectures.

Teacher:	Really?
Ghost:	Clap clap clap. Ask the student about the Weber thesis. Don Quixote.
Teacher:	I mean, I know I got people interested while they were in the lecture, but was there any carry-over?
Student:	Sure. I'm going to read *Don Quixote* over the summer—in Spanish.
Ghost:	You're being told what you want to hear. Or the student is amused by Don Quixote.
Teacher:	What's wrong with being amused? Isn't that the beginning of insight?
Student:	What?
Teacher:	Oh, my ghost wanted me to ask you why you were going to read *Don Quixote* again.
Student:	Well, it's such a great book.
Ghost:	Send the student to the University of Chicago.
Teacher:	How so?
Student:	I mean, here's this man who sees things that are real—or should be real but can't be real because of the world he—no, not he, his friends—live in. Sometimes, I think of myself as a kind of—well, like him. You know, idealistic, saving the world.
Teacher:	Have you given up on saving the world? Why are you going into medicine?
Student:	That's just it! Your class really made me think about that. It blew my mind.
Ghost:	OK, OK, I admit it. You're a fine performer—you can even engineer this conversation so well that the student is unconscious of being manipulated into the right responses.
Teacher:	Not all right responses are untruthful. Can't we be entertained *and* challenged? Why must you be so suspicious of good entertainers within the university, at the same time that you admire drama, good theater, proscenium culture?
Student:	Some ghost!
Teacher:	Oh, sorry again: maybe I should explain. . . . I think that graduate school trains students to be extremely suspicious of teachers who are good performers—who speak well, who know the tricks of timing and drama, who can use large audiences and small audiences just as a skilled actor or actress. You see, in graduate school you learn, supposedly, to be thoughtful and precise and clear of tongue and sharp of eye and . . . right. But good performers take risks, make errors, always verge on being charlatans.

Student: Charlatans?

Ghost: Right, charlatans.

Teacher: Fakes, frauds, people with the proper bluster and no inner truth.

Ghost: Now we are getting somewhere.

Student: Maybe that's why my TA was so dull. I mean, he was very serious and you could see that what he wanted us to know was important to him, but it just never came across.

Teacher: But maybe I spoiled his classes for him by being so flamboyant.

Ghost: Perfect: flame, fireworks, no solid core.

Student: It could be, but you were so wild it was great, we never knew how you would talk about a book and you would come up with something really off the wall, like King Lear and buttons, and after you were done we would all sit there— and it all would make sense.

Teacher: Yes, but didn't that sort of lecturing make you passive in a different way— always waiting for me to think things through for you?

Student: No. You see, because we could never predict what you would say, we began to try to think up the wildest things we could on our own. Like that paper I thought of writing about make-up and cosmetics in Chaucer, *Lear,* and the *Heptameron.*

Ghost: Another Golden Fleece award.

Teacher: Jason was a greater performer.

Ghost: But what truths did he teach?

Teacher: Don't you remember Medea?

Ghost: You touch me to the quick, but remember, I am not... quick.

Teacher: How do ghosts disappear?

Student: Exorcism.

Teacher: Oh, right. . . . Hey, wait a minute, you're going to be a doctor. You believe in exorcism?

Student: No, I guess not. But weren't some of Don Quixote's visions really ghosts? Isn't that why he fought them?

Hillel Schwartz is an instructer in the Department of English, History, and Religious Studies, San Diego State University.

Authentic moments of contact between teacher and student are crucial.

A Teacher's Commentary: Learning from Authentic Moments

Peter Elbow

When I read the foregoing pages and think about teachers learning from teaching I say to myself "authentic moments." Too vague, perhaps, or grand—but at least I do not call them "existential moments." Let me spell out concretely what I mean by authentic moments. And as I do so, let me re-invoke some of these teachers' moments themselves by repeating some lines that continue to ring in my ear. In fact my goal is not just to analyze or interpret but also to create a kind of found poem to try to do justice to the way these writers have managed to tangle authentic moments into their written words. Authentic moments ask us questions:

> "How much effect do I want to have as a teacher?"
> "Reach out to him? ignore him?"
> "Should I try to tell them?"
> "Are you ready to start?"
> "Is it worth the pain?"
> "How did he do it?"
> "Is there anything morally wrong if a student feels fear?"
> "Is that any of my business?"
> "Charlatans?"
> "What are the control signals sent to the kidney?"

W. Martin (Ed.). *New Directions for Teaching and Learning: New Perspectives on Teaching and Learning,* no. 7.
San Francisco: Jossey-Bass, September 1981

But they do not just ask questions. In teaching, perplexity is cheap. Authentic moments often make a dent, make a difference. Something happens.

"I wondered if I should have this much influence" says Michael Schudsen about the effect of his dream assignment on students.

"In several cases, alas, I was too successful" says Patrick Kelly about his efforts to seduce students into seeing Nazism from the inside.

And it is not just to the student that something happens.

"My problem now is to decide whether to change." The moment Byron Nichols presents is not a specific moment in his classroom but his moment alone with himself: it hits him that perhaps he must change his entire approach to teaching, all his assumptions, and give up what he has found the principal satisfactions in the calling itself.

Authentic moments are often times when there is genuine contact between teacher and student. Something happens not just at the cognitive or intellectual level but which involves the whole person.

"Two choices ran through my mind—reach out to him? or ignore him? I climbed over the desks." Sharon Sutton decided she had to break through the architectural barrier her student had erected in her design class— a barrier she sensed he had erected because of her previous teacherly responses to him. She had to respond as a person, not just as a teacher.

"No, not what was Socrates' conception, what *is* the life of virtue? What is it *really?*" James Edwards' student would not accept a teacher's answer, he insisted on a person's answer, and the important moment was a moment of silence. The two people could no longer function as just teacher and student.

"Simply using the container in front of each other within the confines of the small tent would demand an element of frankness and openness; but we thought we could handle that." David Mouw's account of how he and his bride solved their honeymoon camping problem stands inevitably as a metaphor for how he solves his teaching problem: how to use *himself* as a person within the confines of his large impersonal lecture course.

Authentic moments are not planned. They sneak up on us and we find ourselves saying something we had not expected to say, find ourselves with nothing to say, find ourselves having to seize the moment in a way we could have never foreseen.

"The remembrance of this boy's bloody hands and tired eyes made me take a chance." Sharon Sutton had to decide on the spur of the moment. Not to decide would have been to decide. She obviously had not planned to give him his final grade in public, in mid-course, and to give him an A before he had produced his work.

"Too stubborn to adjourn, I fell back on a complicated question about the nature of 'will' that I had not planned to introduce." Peter Manchester had planned twice for this class and two times his plans had been destroyed by external circumstances, and what emerged was impulse.

These authentic moments often have the effect of making us *reperceive* ourselves in a different and sometimes troubling light.

"It approached that vaguely nightmarish experience the psychologists call 'depersonalization,' when it seems like you are watching and listening to yourself as though some stranger, seen from above and behind your own head." Peter Manchester is repelled by the movies of himself inside his head as he tries to lecture about something deeply important to him but something which he had not planned to lecture about.

"In my typical fashion, I continued to point out what was good and what was bad and to say how it could all be improved." As Sharon Sutton stands there before her barricaded architectural student she suddenly reperceives as sour her normal teaching behavior. She is not just having to watch movies of what feels like a blunder, as with Manchester, above. This had always seemed like *good* teaching behavior, but suddenly in this context it rings false to her.

"Most students greatly appreciate what they take as 'honest openness' (which I believe it is). . . . "Dr. Mouw stands out for that uncommon ability to transform even a large classroom with hundreds of students." . . . I have always considered such citations to be largely BS! . . . . Again, it is probably mostly BS, but if there is any truth in it . . . ." Mouw shares his vacillations with us as he is forced to wrestle with two different visions of his teaching: honest, open and ingenuous; but also a calculated performance for planned outcomes.

"Fakes, frauds, people with the proper bluster and no inner truth." Hillel Schwartz precipitates his authentic moment in solitude by writing a dialogue and allowing that ghost to articulate his own worst view of what he nevertheless feels is successful teaching. He is forced to see it both ways.

Authentic moments are often precipitated by the student. The student insists on breaking out of the role of 'student' and rejects the teacher's role as 'teacher.'

"He asked that I read it, commenting that it would help me in the recognition of the truth." Judith Sumner's fundamentalist biology student insists on treating *her* as his student. By "overstepping his bounds" he throws into bold relief what we are often really saying to our students: "I have something important that I really think you ought to know. I realize that you do not believe it and that you do not want to hear it, but it's so important that I must assert my authority and press it on you. You will be grateful later on after you finally understand the truth of what I am saying." This student has the same experience we often have with our students: he uses all his intelligence and assertiveness and yet he fails. His student is unreachable and indeed unrepentant in her unreachableness: "I decided I was a fool ever to become involved in this dialogue."

"I tumbled out some remarks on the Socratic/Platonic conception, dispensing information, but he did not want that: 'No, not what was Socrates' conception, but what *is* the life of virtue? What is it *really*?'" James Edwards' student too is applying to his teacher the technique we so often apply to students. He rejects his teacher's ready answer, he rejects the ideas that grow out of his teacher's assumptions. He forces his teacher into the perplexity that comes from having one's frame of reference violated.

I find myself reflecting at this point on the question of what makes it possible for students to take this role-breaking activity. I'm struck with how Sumner and Edwards did not seem to be teaching in a way that *questioned* their roles. They do not sound like folksy or chummy teachers who say "don't think of me as a teacher, we're all just plain folks in here together." It seems important that they took their roles very seriously indeed, so that at times the shoe did in fact pinch—both student and teacher. Yet that in itself was probably not enough. In addition

Sumner and Edwards must somehow have communicated the sense that it was not out of the question to step out of the roles.

Authentic moments usually involve some risk to us as teachers. And not just the risk that comes from students turning the tables on us or grabbing the reins out of our hand. But also the risk that comes from succeeding—or at least from setting something in motion that surprises us.

> "At first they resisted, but I was after a while quite successful in seducing some of them into seeing [Nazism] from the inside."
>
> "But good performers take risks, make errors, always verge on being charlatans" says Schwartz to the cross-examining ghost.
>
> "Here I had glibly trotted out a phrase—the life of virtue—trading on its power and its deep hold on our hopes, and yet I could not deliver its meaning to this man."

Authentic moments often call upon us for something extra: more than what is fair, more than what we are paid for, more, sometimes, than we have.

> "I could say to him what great thinkers have taken the phrase to encompass but he wanted the truth. I could not deliver."
>
> "I felt that all his rebellion against authority was being dumped on me . . ., and that all his adolescent-male resentment against mothers and women teachers was being directed against me."
>
> "She had come in not to ask for help with a confused lecture, but to seek advice concerning a deeply personal decision she had never been able to parse out for herself, which she said my 'wonderful lecture' had finally illuminated for her."

But I am not trying to define authentic moments precisely. For what seems most important to me about them, in the last analysis, is that they resist classification.

> "This was probably the best course I ever took, but I hate you." This student evaluation of Byron Nichol's course forces him into an intellectual bind.

"Was this learning experience a success or a failure?" "One of the problems with the [Dream] assignment is that in a way it is too good." Kelly and Schudson designed procedures that were so "good" that perhaps they are "bad."

"I wanted to teach this student a sense of responsibility for his own actions. But is that any of my business? What, in fact, did he learn? All I know is that he was angry, abusive, and that I felt uncomfortable and vaguely guilty." Authentic moments can leave you no longer trusting the terms you have been using for deciding whether something is good or bad. They can call your frame of reference into question.

It's interesting to me that when these teachers were asked to describe important moments, they so often came up with moments that defy the categories or schemata they use for classifying experiences. (Sometimes the writer does classify it— David Mouw goes through an impressive classifying process— but usually the moments will not stay put.) One reason these moments come to mind, I presume, is because they don't stay neatly tucked away and understood as concepts. (This suggests the strength of the so-called critical incident technique. It makes us smarter by preventing us from merely using our tired old favorite ideas.)

I am teaching with two others this year in a full-time program called "Humanism and Science." As we wrestle with the question of what these two difficult terms mean an intriguing thought has emerged that bears on these reflections about learning from authentic moments. Science seems always to study and deal with phenomena as instances of a class or a category. Humanists too, of course, look at *To the Lighthouse* or "The Last Supper" or the French Revolution as instances of this or that concept, and rightly so; or try to understand irony or revolution by comparing instances and thereby categorizing better. Nevertheless I'm beginning to think that insofar as I am a humanist I have a special commitment to *moments, single instances, concrete particulars* in and for themselves. Even if cognitive psychologists tell us that we can never see anything in and for itself— that the very act of seeing or understanding necessarily involves seeing each instance as an instance of something else— the fact remains that we *can* feel the difference between the two kinds of seeing. Or at least we can feel the difference between the two ends of the continuum. That is we can feel it when we become hyper-cerebral and lose touch with concrete reality: we begin to live in a world of ideas, classes, concepts; when we speak or write we are only shuffling concepts. And on the other hand we can also feel it when we break out of the web of concepts and see something for itself—experience a moment as an authentic moment. Since the Middle Ages there have been exercises of contemplation to help us get into better contact with unique instances in and for themselves. It may be that the Humanities go awry when they strive *only* to categorize and classify, and forget the need for contemplating concrete particulars in and for themselves.

But even though authentic moments naturally call attention to themselves because they resist classification, it is also a common human response to let them pass unnoticed. We cannot classify them and so we easily let them slide out of mind; or we reperceive them as understandable. Conceptual economy. Wise people become wise, I believe, because they know how to be hospitable to such moments—to savor them. The writers who contributed to this volume help us not only to learn from their moments but also help us become more sensitive to the authentic moments in our own experience. For insofar as we allow authentic moments to remain unclassified, insofar as we resist the impulse to tie them up neatly with a ribbon, they will reward us by somehow being more important than any interpretation of them.

"But what *is* the life of virtue?" James Edwards ends his piece with some intelligent reflections but they are not what I will remember (nor will Edwards either, I bet) but rather the underived question in its experienced context.

It is a relief to realize that we can draw on experiences—return to them and derive authority from them—without always having to understand them.

"One day my wife dragged me to see the movie."

"Too much management, not enough adventure."

"And when it's all said and done I've really enjoyed telling the stories."

*Peter Elbow is a member of the faculty of
Evergreen State College, Olympia, Washington.
His academic specialization is English and
his latest book is Teaching with Power (Oxford
University Press, forthcoming).*

Section 2:
Through Teaching, the Students Learn

A collection of strategies, new techniques, and procedures
to improve teaching is presented in this section.

Introduction

Warren Bryan Martin

Effective teachers are always looking for good strategies and tactics, new techniques and procedures with which to improve their teaching. Here is a collection of such methods, provided in these statements of the moments and incidents that seemed especially illuminating for the teachers who have contributed to this collection.

At a time of criticism, when teaching is said to contribute very little to learning, the statements that follow indicate the power of the interaction between professor and student. More specifically, these statements suggest that when professors teach well, the students learn from that teaching— they learn what is taught and, sometimes, they also learn life's bigger lessons. While it is appropriate to put the emphasis on student learning as the end to which teaching is a means, it is also important to stress that effective teaching— carefully conceptualized, well-organized— makes a difference for the learner.

This section has two main divisions. First, there is a collection of faculty statements dealing with the general organization of a class— ways to structure it, reports of outcomes when innovative procedures are employed, efforts to work with students collectively. Second, there is a group of statements reporting on the teachers' relationships with individual students, the sort of things that happen when the teacher and the learner relate to each other specifically and directly.

W. Martin (Ed.). *New Directions for Teaching and Learning: New Perspectives on Teaching and Learning,* no. 7.
San Francisco: Jossey-Bass, September 1981

Throughout these reports, as they are read separately and then linked together, the reader will notice the numerous ways for teachers to teach so that students will learn. That learning is as varied as the strategies that teachers employ to help bring it about. Both the student's diverse learning and the teacher's developed pedagogy are means to an end, which is the development in the student of a capacity for good judgment. Bartlett Giamatti, President of Yale University, in an article in *Harper's* (July 1980, p. 24), helps us to see how it happens:

> Teaching . . . is about how to make a choice. That is the ethical impulse in teaching— to tell how to go about acquiring the material and then building the edifice of a belief. And from the architectonics of choices, a person will emerge, a person who knows how to cope with the radical loneliness we all inherit and the vast population of decisions we all live in, a person who can carry on.
>
> How we choose to believe, and speak to and treat others, how we choose a civic role for ourselves, is the deepest purpose of a liberal education and of the act of teaching.

So the teacher chooses— subject matter, points of emphasis within the discipline, in other words, *what* will be taught; the teacher chooses the methodology of this inquiry, its strategy and tactics, in other words, *how* to proceed; the teacher chooses the timing, the sequences, the specific chronology of events, in other words, *when* things will come together to form the basis for choice; and, finally, the teacher chooses the gut questions, *why?* and *so what?* These are the questions that figure in the conclusions and inferences for action.

The teacher chooses and the teacher acts, and, working with the student, helps the student develop a capacity for choice and action. Our commitment to this skill, to this service, needs to be kept in mind as we assess the methodologies of the teaching profession.

*One of a teacher's most difficult tasks is passing judgment
on other people in ways that may seriously affect their lives.*

Discipline About Deadlines

John B. Taylor

A girl who as a freshman had done only slightly better than average
work for me in a year of introductory political science came to me as a
sophomore to ask if she could take my course in American Constitutional Law. She had completed the prerequisites, but her academic
adviser was highly skeptical of her ability to handle this demanding
course, and he had grudgingly agreed to approve her enrollment only if
I consented. She insisted that she wanted to try something challenging,
and I gave my permission. When she scored only a 72 on the first test,
however, she came to me again, quite dispirited, and announced that
if she were really not succeeding then she wanted to drop the course. I
persuaded her to stick it out through one more exam. We were both
pleasantly surprised when she scored an 86 and went on to do solid
"B" work for the rest of the semester, including the writing of a good
term paper on the equal rights amendment, about which she became
both intellectually and emotionally excited.

Although this sequence of events turned out to be one of my
most gratifying experiences as a teacher (and, I believe, one of her
most satisfying experiences as a student), I am struck by how problem-
atical the outcome was at many points. In the first place, this girl's
enrollment in Constitutional Law would have occurred as a matter of
course, had her adviser not made an issue of it. He was a mathematician

W. Martin (Ed.). *New Directions for Teaching and Learning: New Perspectives on Teaching and Learning,* no. 7.
San Francisco: Jossey-Bass, September 1981

who was bright, personable, and conscientious, but he was totally unable to adjust his performance down to the level of our students, and he was not rehired. I think he acted quite properly, in the best interests of his advisees as he perceived them, but that perception was necessarily based only on academic records and a few short personal conferences. Another advisor in similar circumstances might have talked this girl right out of taking my course or might have routinely enrolled another student who definitely should not have taken the course. This adviser no doubt did the right thing by raising the question and then deferring to my judgment (if only because I happened to know her better), but the incident does point up the inherent limitations of academic advising.

Second, why were this girl's qualifications in question? Since she had done only mediocre work as a freshman, in relatively easy courses, it appeared that she just was not a very good student. Later in her senior year, however, after having successfully completed yet another advanced course with me, she confided that she had simply been bored at the introductory level. How to distinguish the good student one has failed to arouse from the poor one who is already doing his best? The student who should be taken at her word when she says she needs a challenge from the one who needs to be deterred from getting in over her head? Neither her advisor nor I was sure, and I do not think either one of us made the distinction very explicitly at the time. (The best solution, obviously, is to present stimulating introductory courses, but I have encountered no more intractable problem in teaching.)

Third, why did I react as I did in my two key conferences with this student? I initally allowed her to enroll because she clearly wanted to, because I felt she could probably struggle through, because I was not then sufficiently confident of my ability as a teacher or of the security of my employment to contemplate turning away students with equanimity, and because I am a soft touch at heart. I thus clearly made the right decision for a variety of good and not-so-good reasons. I might as easily have turned away this student who did rise to the challenge or have admitted one who would have fallen into serious academic difficulty, creating a drag on the rest of the class in the process. Later, I encouraged her to stick it out a little longer because the withdrawal deadline allowed it and she had caught me by surprise. (The prospect of a "C" had given me no pause at all, but it was very unsettling to her.) Without deeply believing it, I made the standard response: This course presents unfamiliar material and introduces an unfamiliar mode of reasoning. It ususally requires a considerable adjustment for many students, and the first exam is typically an eye-opener. Why not give it one more try and see what happens? I did not want her to drop the course; I felt that would be bad for her and look bad for me. So once again, I made the right move for uncertain reasons. Conscientiously considering both this student's welfare and the necessity to maintain standards in advanced courses, I might as easily have advised her to bail out.

Ironically, this most heartening teaching experience has taught me not so much about the determinants of success as about the fragility of it. One of the most difficult of a teacher's responsibilities—psychologically, more so than intellectually—is the necessity of passing judgment on other people in ways that may seriously affect the course of their lives. He can evaluate their work on the basis of reasonably straightforward professional standards, but in assessing students' innate capacities and current needs, does a teacher have much more to go on than his own experience and intuition? Is this part of the reason why the ability to teach well has generally been considered to be an intangible quality? If either of my key decisions about this student had been wrong, I would never have known it. Can we help each other to sense such things?

John B. Taylor is an associate professor in the Department of Political Science and International Studies at Washington College, Chestertown, Maryland.

Drama comes into a classroom in a teacher's
spontaneous return to her student acting days.

A Dramatic Experience

Margaret O'Gara

My professor of Shakespeare was a dignified, middle-aged English woman whose lectures were always delivered from a fully written text that had been carefully prepared. She was considered the best lecturer in the college, yet she once confessed to me that she had never overcome the feeling of nervousness that plagued her before each lecture. During one class, she realized suddenly that a particularly difficult point about one of the comedies could not be communicated merely by explanation. She put down her text, stepped aside from the podium, and launched into reciting and acting the parts of the three characters we were studying. More clearly than any explanation, her performance illumined for her students the significance of the difficult passage. Her personal passion for Shakespeare and his work had set us on fire. Her performance seemed even more skillful to me when I learned later that it had not been planned, simply recalled from student acting days at Oxford. I would like to be a teacher like that, whose personal involvement in her subject allowed her to respond spontaneously in the way best suited for her students' learning.

Margaret O'Gara is on the faculty of theology at St. Michael's College, University of Toronto.

W. Martin (Ed.). *New Directions for Teaching and Learning: New Perspectives on Teaching and Learning,* no. 7.
San Francisco: Jossey-Bass, September 1981

A shift in teaching strategy moves the professor away from being the primary "font of knowledge" to having the students take much larger and more active learning responsibilities.

An Alternative Way of Organizing a Class

John McClusky

I have journeyed from traditional to alternative college teaching. In my traditional phase, I was a political scientist teaching separate courses for three to four semester hours credit in discrete subject areas of political theory, my specialization. The course enrollments ranged from 12 to 200 students, depending on whether they were advanced graduate seminars or introductory undergraduate classes.

In my alternative phase, I instruct and facilitate student learning in a 10.5 semester-hour, integrated set of subjects in a "cluster group," which never exceeds eight students. We meet once a week for three to five hours per session, and the students come prepared to give oral presentations on topics, as well as to participate intensively in group discussions about common readings and reactions to my presentations. Students take a single cluster group as their entire trimester of study; skipping around among curricular "fragments" by studying three to five separate courses each term is not allowed. Students average about fifteen to twenty hours of independent study outside of the cluster sessions each week, reading extensively, preparing oral presentations, researching and writing papers and conducting field projects. They also meet in occasional tutorial sessions with a faculty adviser who

W. Martin (Ed.). *New Directions for Teaching and Learning: New Perspectives on Teaching and Learning*, no. 7. San Francisco: Jossey-Bass, September 1981

helps them formulate individualized study plans and reviews and critiques their research and writing skills.

I am going to describe some moments from the cluster group I taught in the second trimester after I had joined this alternatie program. The cluster was studying the politics (and to a lesser degree economics) of voluntary organizations and the voluntary sector. This is one of four trimesters of required subjects in a bachelor's and master's degree program in the administration of voluntary organizations, which I direct. Within general curriculum guidelines regarding student requirements (give at least two oral presentations, write at least two major papers, and so forth), subject matter outlines, and cluster group process, students have extensive freedom to formulate their individual and group learning objectives.

Faced with this exciting but novel teaching situation, I set several major goals. These included achieving a balance among three modes of teaching-learning: didactic instruction by the faculty member, instruction through oral presentations by the individual students, and intensive group discussion and dialogue. I wanted students to participate extensively in the cluster sessions as colearners, bearers and sharers of knowledge, skills, methodologies, experiences.

Immediately, this meant I had to alter my former teaching style in which I was the primary "font" of knowledge (which had been true even though I emphasized discussion along with lecture in my former classes). Now I actively encouraged students' presentation of their ideas and leadership of group discussion, at times letting the students interact among themselves for fifteen to twenty minutes without my intervention. Additionally, students were giving oral presentations in which they were the instructors for twenty minutes or an hour. We evolved into a pattern in which we had roughly a third of the session devoted to my presentations and ensuing discussion, a third to individual student presentations and ensuing discussion, and a third to group discussions of common readings or group learning exercises, such as problem solving, role playing, simulations, or other experiences. For example, we organized ourselves as a mock board of a voluntary organization while a student took on the role of a staff person trying to persuade the board to undertake a new political or service program. Such an exercise would be done in conjunction with readings on the dynamics of power and communications within organizations.

One particular student presentation that trimester illustrates this approach. A student gave an oral presentation on community power structures, comparing the pluralist and elitist positions and applying them to a major urban policy issue in St. Louis (where all the students live). The student researched and organized her presentation beautifully. She brought out major views from these conflicting positions and examined how the political history of this issue— whether or not to build a freeway through the inner city— exemplified aspects of both positions. Students were reading Bachrach and Baratz, *Power and Poverty,* a well as individually selected sources on the general subject of community power. The student delivered her presentation with succinctness and clarity, accompanied by excellent visual aids she had prepared. This was one of the first student presentations for the trimester (I had steered the schedule to the extent that I asked her to be one of the early presenters) and set an example for other students about its potential. This presentation came after the cluster had been meeting a couple of hours, on an evening after students had put in full workdays. (They are all adults employed in some capacity in nonprofit and voluntary organizations.) Their energy and enthusiasm were a sight to behold.

I could have given a lecture on the same topic, but several things would not have happened. Students would not have had the encouraging (but not arrogant or intimidating) example of one of their peers giving a superb presentation. They would not have learned in such rich, perceptive detail about a major policy issue in their community and its power structure. They would never have had the visual learning stimuli in addition to the auditory ones. (I cultivate that skill in others, but do not practice it much myself beyond using an easel or chalkboard.) They would not have had the peer model of how to understand, analyze, and apply difficult conceptual material (on power, power structures, and political process) to a real-life case from their community. And they would not have had the change of pace and learning stimulus that comes from presentations by different persons, each with a unique presentation of self in everyday life.

I have thought to myself on this and numerous other occasions in these clusters, "I'm really learning to relax about not being the primary font of knowledge and wisdom for students." I no longer assume that if I do not give them one of my "superb" lectures, or lead the discussion about a topic, they will not learn enough or properly about it. I can then build upon student presentations to develop critiques of leading positions or alternative perspectives on topics. And I have become much more attentive to verbal and nonverbal signs of interest, restlessness, and energy in teaching. The mutual support, intensity, and excitement that most of the students exhibit in engaging in teaching-learning in these clusters have made this as fulfilling a professional experience for me as any.

70

John McClusky is Executive Director of the Coro Foundation, St. Louis, Missouri.

*There is a tide in the affairs of students that taken at its crest
leads on to learning*

Teaching and the Quality of Time

James Herbert

It has always seemed to me that knowing how to present knowledge to
students required understanding what students are already thinking.
One valuable way of achieving this understanding is to be aware of the
circumstances in which students are doing their thinking. An important aspect of those circumstances is what I have come to think of as the
rhythms of their semester. It is useful to keep these rhythms in mind as
the course proceeds, but it is even more effective to anticipate them
while planning the syllabus for a course. Since these rhythms vary
from place to place, there is no substitute for a teacher's actual
experience on his own campus.

To academic planners, a contact hour is usually just a contact
hour. To scholars, a sequence of fifteen weeks can look like the number
of units into which a logical exposition of their topic can be divided. But
teachers come to realize that a lot more learning takes place in some
weeks than in other weeks.

In planning a syllabus I first try to take into account the overall
schedule of campus activities likely to engage or distract students'
energies: preparing for and returning from holidays, the pressure of
exams and papers in other courses, basketball tournaments, student
elections, and so on. Then I try to think about when students get
involved in courses, and when they begin to turn their enthusiasm to

W. Martin (Ed.). *New Directions for Teaching and Learning: New Perspectives on Teaching and Learning*, no. 7.
San Francisco: Jossey-Bass, September 1981

anticipating the next semester. The first weeks of the semester involve a natural building up of steam and the last weeks a sort of decompression. I try to schedule the most challenging, rewarding, and important readings or topics for the weeks when the students have become comfortable with the course but when their enthusiasm for it is still very high. In my experience, this has meant that the third, fourth, and fifth weeks of the semester account for about forty percent of the actual learning in the course. By careful attention to breaks and diversions it is possible to allow for a second burst of excellence around the tenth and eleventh weeks. I have always regarded this second wind as bonus, when the course can achieve much more than can normally be expected. To scramble sports metaphors, arranging a syllabus seems like planning a batting line-up. The heavy hitters go in the third, fourth, and fifth slots. This is because teaching is like coaching basketball. The game has internal rhythms which are far more important than the regular sequence of minutes on the clock.

Each class has its own special rhythms, and each student his own ups and downs within the group. The experienced teacher learns to adjust to, and make the most of, these special qualities. But the variable quality of students' time seems one of the circumstances which teachers need to understand.

For a while the vogue was to regard the syllabus as a learning contract agreed to at the beginning of the course by teacher and students. This never worked for me. At the beginning of the semester my students were in no mood to negotiate contracts with a stranger. By the time they were ready to engage in such negotiations, the course was already well under way. I have found it useful, however, to ask students to reorganize the syllabus at the end of the semester, looking back on their own experience and forward to the likely experience of other students. In this sense, the syllabus can be considered a contract, a contract, as Edmund Burke said, between generations. This is part of the reason I think that teaching is above all a tradition of practical wisdom.

James Herbert is the director of the Study of Governance and Education at the Carnegie Foundation for the Advancement of Teaching, Washington, D. C.

Field study experience raises the question of the limitations classroom courses place upon students.

Fieldwork as a Learning Experience

Mary Grey Osterud

The seminar came to Old Sturbridge Village for a three-day field study on women's roles in early nineteenth-century New England. They had been reading American literature by and about women and looking at paintings of women and families. The field study in the museum was intended to provide them with an historical context in which to place these works and an experiential framework within which to interpret them.

　　Throughout the field study, the students used past and present to illuminate one another. They moved easily back and forth between their activities in the museum—exploring a living historical farm, preparing a meal over the hearth, reading women's diaries and letters—and their contemporary lives. They contrasted the economic marginality of housework today with its centrality to the farm family economy and traced continuities in the repetitive yet constantly interrupted quality of women's daily working lives. They considered how women's work might have shaped the way others saw them and the way they saw and felt about themselves. Using their own understandings of family relationships, they speculated about sources of unity and tension in family life in the early nineteenth century.

W. Martin (Ed.). *New Directions for Teaching and Learning: New Perspectives on Teaching and Learning*, no. 7.
San Francisco: Jossey-Bass, September 1981

When they returned to the college, they were asked to write something that related the field study to the material they had been working with in the seminar. These papers proved to be dismal failures. The students either produced formal, academic papers that had no connection to the field experience or wrote intensely personal descriptions of that experience that had nothing to do with the material of the course itself. Their ability to relate past and present, themselves and the subject mattter, had disappeared in the transition from museum to campus.

The students said that the field study was the best educational experience they had had in their college careers. But it was impossible for them to articulate the meaning and value of that experience, at least within the terms that were available to them as students. Some recognized the problem, appending statements such as "this paper doesn't really reflect what happened to me at Old Sturbridge Village" to the written work they submitted.

Why is it so difficult for students to find a voice that is authentically personal, yet seriously engaged with the material they are studying? How can teachers help them do in the classroom what came naturally to them in the museum setting?

Mary Grey Osterud lives in Binghamton, New York.

Playing with language provides a smash hit as well as a way of learning French.

A Daring Experiment

Gail Hilary Nigrosh

This year I taught an elementary college-level French course for students who had some previous exposure to the language but who had not advanced very far, even though some had had as much as three or four years of French in high school. The idea was to give them a fresh start, to get them to see that language need not be learned only through the set dialogues and pattern drills that most of them had experienced. I wanted them to see that rules of language are not the end but the means for creative language use. I wanted them to play with language.

Early in the first semester, we hit a unit in the textbook that concentrated on terms for parts of the body, articles of clothing, and colors, none of which was too exciting to the students or me. I was looking for a way to bring the new expressions to life in some memorable context, so I told the class we could have a fashion show with commentary—*un véritable défilé de mode*—very Parisian, after all. A great chorus of "yechh!" greeted my suggestion, until I explained that this would not be the corny event they all envisioned. Rather, this would be super corny.

I divided the class into groups and gave each a task unknown to the others. One group would make costumes using only articles found in the kitchen. Another would dress all in black and describe fantastic

W. Martin (Ed.). *New Directions for Teaching and Learning: New Perspectives on Teaching and Learning*, no. 7. San Francisco: Jossey-Bass, September 1981

clothes that were not there—a modest version of "The Emperor's New Clothes." One group would do an outrageous takeoff on the Color Trak TV commercials—"My hair is blue, my hat is red, and my teeth are vivid green." A group of women would form a chorus line wearing one costume on the left side of their bodies and another on the right. This left one large contingent of very tough guys, still glaring at me in disgust, hoping that looks really could kill. In desperation, I told them they would all be John Travolta.

My role, at this point, had been only to give the class the rules of play. The strategies they devised, the way they played would be uniquely theirs. The group structure, I hoped, would give individuals, both timid and outspoken, the support they needed to take some creative chances. Mostly, I hoped that they would enjoy—and retain—what they learned in this way. In the following class, I reviewed each group's script to make sure that the French was well chosen and that there were no major problems with pronunciation. The Travoltas refused my assistance.

On the day of our *grand spectacle*—which happened to fall on Halloween—the skits were presented with more imagination and humor than I could have ever brought to the project. The Travoltas had asked to be last, as they assured me that nothing could follow their act. Finally, they were on.

The first Travolta burst through the door in T-shirt, jeans and sneakers, announcing, in perfect French overlaid with a Brooklyn accent, "Moi, je suis John Travolta." He was followed by six others, identically dressed, each insisting that he was John Travolta. The first reinforced his claim, pointing to his white T-shirt, "Moi, je suis John Travolta parce que j'ai un T-shirt blanc." The six others made the same claim, "because I have a white T-shirt," adding blue jeans and sneakers on successive rounds. The first then produced his leather jacket. The others did the same. He put on his sunglasses. So did they. The seven Travoltas began to quarrel, pushing and shoving each other and tossing out insults (in good French).

This, they had told me, would be my signal to start a tape recorder that they had given me. The theme music from the film "Saturday Night Fever" came up. The door opened again, and in walked the eighth Travolta in white three-piece suit. "Silence," he ordered, then said, with perfect authority, "Moi, je suis John Travolta parce que moi, j'ai la fille," whereupon a young woman, not even a member of the class, appeared in disco dress and the two of them danced out the door, leaving the other Travoltas crushed. End of skit, end of class. They had been right. Nothing could follow them.

What made me feel so good about that class was the confidence and the joy with which the students had taken center stage and become their own teachers. I feel best about teaching when the people in my classes assume leading roles and I can be a less visible player. With the Travoltas, I felt like a good producer who have given the actors enough backing to make their own show. That day we had a Broadway hit. Some days we bomb in Philadelphia.

Gail Hilary Nigrosh is lecturer in French at Clark University, Worcester, Massachusetts.

*Diversity in the classroom may be rewarding to the teacher,
but it may reveal that students are reluctant to learn from
each other.*

Diversity in the Classroom:
Pro and Con

Charles Rearick

It looked like a ideal teaching situation for a history course—fifteen
students, one evening session for about two hours each week, and a fresh
subject that I was particularly interested in. There would be plenty of
opportunity for discussion, which all of us lecture-weary students of
history would appreciate. The readings were rich and diverse: some,
like J. H. Plumb, entertainingly describing cultural changes in a
colorful and not obviously political way; others, E. P. Thompson and
Harry Brewerman, fired with critical moral and political feeling and
judgment. The students would have to make their own judgments, not
just because the readings took different points of view, but also because
my essay questions required them to present their own conclusions.

 The class members turned out to be the most interesting
assortment of students I have taught: several older students who
wanted to learn and who had no concern at all for grades, credits, and
other matters of academic ritual; an engineering student and a plant-
and-soil-science major who found history courses a welcome diversion;
a business student whose true preference was the humanities; and
some history majors—a couple of underclassmen who evidently still
hoped to learn everything about the past and two seniors who had

W. Martin (Ed.). *New Directions for Teaching and Learning: New Perspectives on Teaching and Learning*, no. 7.
San Francisco: Jossey-Bass, September 1981

taken enough history courses to make them little interested in more details, blasé about more historical reading in general, but strong in their convictions about the workings of history.

One of the early difficult times for me occurred when I was discussing peasant work and changes in farming known as the "agricultural revolution." The pens of diligent history majors were scurrying across their notebooks; some of the students pressed for details: What was "marling"? "In what countries were open fields the rule?" Several of the older students impatiently awaited the verdict: enclosures? The capitalists needed laborers in the new factories; it is all simply capitalism. Later the first essays confirmed my impression of the students' selective receptivity. Some papers meandered through details on agricultural innovations; others concentrated on how once free and happy peasants were victimized by capitalists on the land and in factory villages. In a general eagerness to portray the hell of factory life, all the notes on the dismal side of peasant life were lost.

By the time we reached the topic of Taylorism late in the semester, positions had hardened as academic fatigue and spring fever took their toll. One of the most vocal and ideological students who also was clearly not reading assigned books launched into a discourse on the workings of the multinational corporations. If only he had read Braverman or Haber's nuanced, non-Marxist analysis of Taylor, he could have connected his remarks with the common reading. I was giving him a chance to say his piece and hoping to tie in something that he said with the assigned books. At one point, several students began to argue with the rambling speaker, unfortunately not with much knowledge and not with reference to material covered by the course. It was clear to me anyway that personal irritations and personality conflicts were more involved than differences of opinions.

For me the diversity of the class was rewarding. One student—a carpenter, a 1960s counterculture veteran—could speak more knowledgeably of the craftsman's life and work than I could. An economics major with much grounding in Marxist thought unknowingly prodded me toward more critical thinking. My discussions with a nonacademic Vietnam veteran (who still has an "incomplete" for the course) helped me to focus on the large questions. My disappointment is that the students did not learn more from each other. For some, complexities and qualifications were simply bothersome, unnecessary detail, quickly forgotten if ever learned. Yet I wonder: Will those who so readily cast history into villains and victims remember more in the end than those who immersed themselves in the complex, detailed accounts and took "balanced" positions? Why are students not more open to other students' views? Discussions can degenerate into shibboleths and personality conflicts, but I do not want to strong-arm students into developing points that I have in mind.

Charles Rearick is an associate professor in the Department of History at the University of Massachusetts, Amherst.

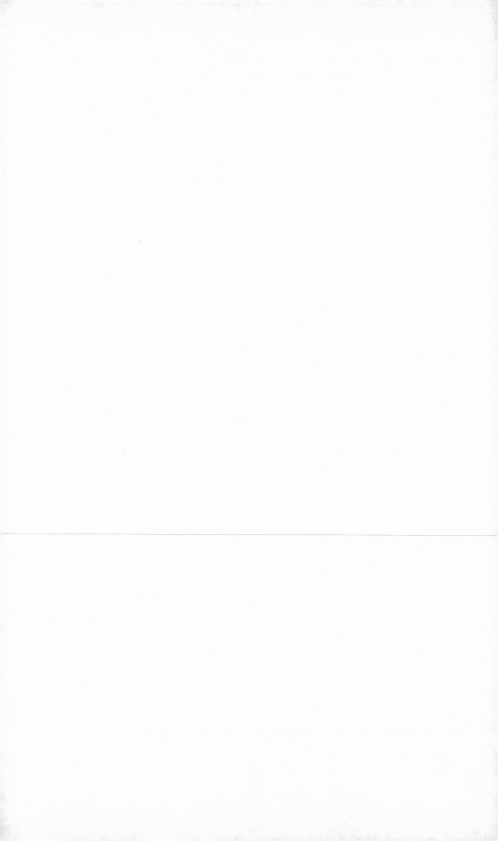

*A teacher finds that highly personalized learning can be
stimulating but also politically threatening.*

Radical Change and Its Effects

Sally Adair Rigsbee

I teach in the English department of a small, church-related women's
college in the Southeast. For nearly a century, the traditions have
included striving for respectable academic standards and providing a
protected social environment for the female offspring of a conservative
but loyal constituency. In the last decade, student demands have
eliminated the strict social control that once characterized dormitory
life, and now students can do whatever state university students can
except drink and entertain men in their rooms. The expanded social
freedom was accompanied by a desire for greater academic indepen-
dence. The college approved a "special studies" program that allowed
any student, group of students, or faculty member to create a course,
provided they could get the approval of a department chairman and the
dean. Early in the 1970s the college president appointed a committee
of women faculty to write a women's studies proposal, which was subsequently awarded $100,000 in grants from Mellon and Rockefeller.
The president also appointed the college's first female administrator.

Meanwhile, in the midst of this progressive atmosphere, students in my department were struggling for a broader curriculum. For
many years, English majors have taken twenty-one hours in prescribed
courses for the thirty-hour major: two British literature survey courses,

W. Martin (Ed.). *New Directions for Teaching and Learning: New Perspectives on Teaching and Learning,* no. 7.
San Francisco: Jossey-Bass, September 1981

Old English, Chaucer, Milton, and two semesters of Shakespeare. Granted, the firmly traditional program serves prospective graduate students well, but general students, prospective high school teachers, majors, other faculty, and the dean were consistently requesting more American and modern literature, genre and thematically based courses, interdisciplinary, theatre, and film courses—an English program more relevant to modern life. Out of a firm belief in the superiority of a traditional program and her personal fear of passing "fads," the department chairman refused to make even the slightest alteration in the curriculum. Furthermore, the chairman advocated a kind of "Paper Chase" approach to education—fear and scolding produce disciplined, achieving students who later deeply appreciate their teachers' concern.

I came to the college in 1972 with the same social and religious background of most of its students and faculty, and with training in English of the James Moffett variety—an emphasis on student interests, thoughts, behaviors, and needs and a focus on developing skills and concepts rather than on propagating the superiority of certain literary figures or periods. In this particular institutional setting, I experienced a kind of "snowballing" success in stimulating excitement about learning and in broadening the personal and educational horizons of students.

The process began in a survey course: students responded with enthusiasm to the concepts of personal self-reliance and self-esteem advocated by Emerson, Thoreau, and Whitman and then confronted the inhibited lives of the characters in *Winesburg, Ohio*. They began to understand in a new way the frustrations they saw in their mothers. Dormitory discussions brought students back to me with repeated requests for informal literary groups to extend the semester's study and with proposals for special studies courses. From a core of three, then fifteen and eventually nearly a hundred different students, a series of new courses was born. I got permission to offer for the first time an elective in the American novel, and over thirty students enrolled. The students proposed a "special studies" course on Creativity—readings included *Portrait of the Artist* and fiction by D. H. Lawrence, works not previously taught in the department, as well as Maslow, Rollo May, Jung, and Neumann on theories of the creative unconscious. The question of creative potential led us to the women's movement, and with support from the women's studies grant we created a film course, Female Identity. Nine feature-length films—among them, "La Strada," "Scenes from a Marriage," "A Free Woman," "Face to Face"—along with readings from *Adam Bede* and *Madame Bovary* to *Fear of Flying*— raised stimulating and disturbing issues. The long-awaited film course brought a new learning problem, dealing with subtitles. Coping with frustrations of adult women who took the course through continuing education was a more serious ordeal.

Learning was becoming personalized, intriguing, but sometimes painful. Facing the prospects of a divorce myself, I found the highly personalized learning I was experiencing with my students the most stimulating teaching I had done, but also a frightening "boundary" situation—I had no models and no guides to either the content or the methods of instruction. I became persuaded that learning and teaching are a very different kind of experience for women, for nothing in my college education, conducted entirely by males, had prepared me for the learning and teaching unfolding in myself and my students. Only a handful of my colleagues seemed to understand either the material or the intense involvement and excitement generated among the students. Finally, through a grant for interdisciplinary seminars, a course emerged with readings in psychology, religion, and literature, along with films on altered states of consciousness, fantasy and myth (Cocteau's "Orpheus" and "Beauty and the Beast"), and mysticism. Our own "boundary" educational experience had led to the study of boundary experiences of the mind. That semester a colleague in psychology taught a course in science fiction and invited me to teach a literary work each semester in his personality course.

A new rapport had developed among some students and some faculty. Students' ideas spread to other courses and other departments A large number of students and I experienced a sense of genuinely broadened horizons. Participants in the courses went on to prestigious graduate schools, traveled widely, became active feminists, explored unusual life styles; I know of none who are "trapped" in traditional roles, but new problems have emerged for some. The flow of ideas and the freedom to expand to new courses and to merge disciplines led to an experience of spontaneity and sheer joy in learning.

All in all, an exciting educational experience, but not without its dark side. The content of the courses and the enthusiasm of the students were threatening to many faculty members. Although I felt genuinely appreciated by the administration and some colleagues, becoming labeled an intellectual radical did not enhance my position in my department. I offered every special studies course except the last one as an addition to my regular twelve-hour load and severely overextended myself to avoid slighting my other courses or assigned committee work. "Personalizing" education led me into intimate involvement with several students in "heavy" counseling situations, making me feel for a while that I badly needed the training of a psychologist to be an adequate teacher. Throughout the three-year period, I had to struggle with my department chairman for permission to teach each new course. Only later did I realize the hazards of offering special studies courses, which take away enrollment from more traditional courses. I learned, sadly enough, that many professional educators find excitement and stimulation in learning so undesirable and frightening that they will actively discourage it. Granting a great deal of time and energy to innovative teaching that is responsive to the needs of students may not enhance one's academic career; I certainly had no time left for publication nor did I win the approval of my chairman.

Sally Adair Rigsbee is an instructor in the Department of English at Meredith College, Raleigh, North Carolina.

*An assumption that incoming freshman students would
catch an ironic tone nearly sabotages a teacher's best
intentions.*

An Essential Ingredient: Irony

John Tallmadge

I teach several "core courses" in the liberal education program. The
clientele for these courses is largely made up of freshmen who want to
get their general requirements out of the way before taking up their
majors, so each class is quite a mixture of backgrounds, intellectual
abilities and interests. Last fall, my section of the Problems in Human
Values Course focused on wilderness and the ethics of land use, with
reading assignments from the works of American naturalists and
explorers.

One day we were discussing Aldo Leopold's *Sand County
Almanac,* a collection of subtle and bittersweet essays celebrating the
delights of wildlife. The essays all seemed transparently clear to me,
making their points with subtle but powerful Thoreauian irony. Yet the
class did not seem to respond; try as I might I could not seem to
generate a discussion, though previous texts had proved stimulating
enough. After two days of fruitless probing, I became irritated and
impatient; I chastised the class for not paying more attention to the
reading, and they stonewalled me.

That afternoon one of the better students, an older woman who
had returned to complete her degree, came to my office and confessed
that she had not understood a word of Leopold's book. She hoped I
was not offended, but she had wrestled with the book for several days

W. Martin (Ed.). *New Directions for Teaching and Learning: New Perspectives on Teaching and Learning,* no. 7.
San Francisco: Jossey-Bass, September 1981

and others in the class whom she had talked with were apparently having the same problem. I was shocked, for to me the book seemed unmistakably clear. But I soon realized that the class had simply missed the point: they had failed to notice the irony. The next day, I took the class through a word-by-word reading of the first essay; after that, they all became quite interested and we began to have lively discussions.

I feel as if I came within a hair's breadth of losing that class. If that student had not come to see me, I never would have thought to undertake such an elementary close reading. Perhaps I never should have assumed that incoming freshmen really know how to read, but how can you know where to pitch your presentations when your classes represent such a heterogeneous mix?

John Tallmadge is an assistant professor of English at Carleton College, Northfield, Minnesota.

The questions students ask are often disconcertingly beside the point of a teacher's efforts, but nonetheless revealing.

Modern Manners

Albert S. Furtwangler

Sometimes I find myself struggling with modern manners. This is usually outside of class, in a hurried moment, when a student wants something that I would never have thought of asking:

"You the one that teaches the Bible and all that old junk?"

"You have neat ideas in class and I was wondering— I have this skit I have to do for a pajama party next week and maybe you could give me some suggestions."

"I know *you* don't give me good marks on my work, but I've been talking it over with the assistant to the dean, and she doesn't think that it's so bad."

I have learned to listen in neutral and try to detect a point on which a neutral answer can be made. But such questions always put me in a false position. To accept their tone is false. To avoid a direct answer is false. To make an elaborate or "now look here" answer is false, too. Often the student is struggling to find his bearings and he is addressing me with something besides hostility. Each failure in these encounters buzzes in my head for a week.

Albert S. Furtwangler teaches English at Mount Allison University, Sackville, New Brunswick, Canada.

W. Martin (Ed.). *New Directions for Teaching and Learning: New Perspectives on Teaching and Learning*, no. 7. San Francisco: Jossey-Bass, September 1981

Plagiarism or suspected plagiarism poses as many dilemmas
for the teacher as for the student.

Plagiarism

Maud Gleason

I had some problems with plagiarism this year, and I took it very hard. One student in my undergraduate humanities section handed me a paper on Roman slavery that contained no grammatical mistakes. The essay was not well organized or focused, but the sentences that composed it were well written. This must have made me suspicious since the student was neither thoughtful nor articulate in class. He was the sort of kid who asks the teacher for a one-sentence definition of stoicism to transcribe into his notebook for the exam. My suspicions intensified when I recognized a paragraph I had read somewhere before—in a book I had recommended to him.

Having determined that the essay was indeed a jumble of lifted paragraphs I phoned the professor for whom I was teaching, and he said he would take care of it. But the next day the student came to my office and asked how to make his paper better (rewriting was part of the exercise). I asked rhetorically, "Do you know what plagiarism is?" He maintained ignorance. Stonewalled. Sullenly refused to admit wrongdoing. But if he had been innocent, would he not have been offended? protested indignantly? His eyes seemed to me shifty, but perhaps he was nervous and shy. He had terrible acne—did that make me misjudge him? I was convinced he was lying. What to do next? He was a senior in economics and very scared. I think he must have had

W. Martin (Ed.). *New Directions for Teaching and Learning: New Perspectives on Teaching and Learning,* no. 7. San Francisco: Jossey-Bass, September 1981

some difficulty mustering the grades to graduate. He had probably plagiarized his way with varying success through three and one-half years. Who was going to get through to him now? We could get nowhere until he admitted he had cheated deliberately. Then we could have talked abut his fears: his low competence? my high standards? But he sullenly maintained he did not know it was plagiarism to compose an entire essay by cutting unacknowledged paragraphs out of other people's books. I hesitated to challenge him because I did not trust my own instincts; I was afraid I was prejudiced; I wanted to take the student at his word. But since I was not satisfied that he was telling me the truth, should I have pressed the matter? I do not think he learned anything from the impasse except more fear.

I learned to be harsher, more suspicious. When Mark, a soft-spoken freshman with a slightly foreign accent, gave me a paper that was mostly *Horizon Book of Ancient Rome* I did not ask rhetorical questions. I told him that it had made me suspicious of everyone's work to find one piece plagiarized. I cannot possibly check the *Horizon* books for fifty papers. I have to trust students. I am here to help them write better and will spend hours with any student whose work is his or her own. Long before I had finished this tirade, the look on Mark's face began to hurt me. I could see that he was listening very seriously; the young eyes above the ski jacket shone with still tears. The only thing that kept me going was that I wanted this person to learn to protect his integrity while he was still young. This is how parents must feel, I remember thinking, when they cause hurt because they love.

Mark's paper went through several drafts and we spent a lot of time over it, working well together. Just before finals he told me that his father had been killed in a plane crash in South Africa. Very self-contained, he finished the quarter. There was not anything he wanted me to do, but perhaps because we had lived through the plagiarism episode together, there was a basis for empathy. He never finished the section on Roman funeral customs.

Maud Gleason is a teaching assistant in the Department of Classics at the University of California, Berkeley.

There are times when the teacher can help students transcend the damage cause by acts of plagiarism.

"Will You Help Me?"

Andre Guerrero

I had questioned the integrity of one of my most promising graduate students. He had been a migrant worker himself and knew the special problems faced by Hispanic children who moved so frequently that continuity of schooling was impossible. The curriculum that he had designed, in Spanish, for teaching reading to migrant children, bore an uncomfortable resemblance to several books I had seen in Mexico, and I told him so. Had portions of his work been "borrowed"? If so, why was credit not given the original author? I asked him to prepare an explanation of the similarities in the two works, and notified his committee that his Master's orals would have to be postponed. My sense of the situation was that he had copied someone else's work, and that this was sufficient cause for requesting his withdrawal from the degree program.

After he told me he had copied portions of the work, I was completely unprepared for his question. "What do you want me to do?" I did not know what I wanted him to do. "Design another reading program, and make it better than the version you copied from," I told him. "Will you help me?" he asked. Yes, I would help him. He graduated from our program, went on for his doctorate, and is now spoken of with respect by others in his field. This was the first time I had compromised a standard of excellence that I felt should not be compromised. When

W. Martin (Ed.). *New Directions for Teaching and Learning: New Perspectives on Teaching and Learning,* no. 7.
San Francisco: Jossey-Bass, September 1981

94

should standards be enforced? How? At what expense? This experience was an introduction to dilemmas that seem to be occurring with more frequency than I would like.

Andre Guerrero has been director of the Commission on Spanish-Speaking Affairs, Columbus, Ohio.

*Students can experience transformations that defy
a teacher's early and often pessimistic expectations.*

Margy the "Outlaw" Goes Straight

Bruce Breland

Margy is a very bright student, daughter of an outstanding dean at an
Eastern Ivy League campus, a faculty "brat." She was an obvious misfit
in a professional school curriculum— talented enough, but not willing
to conform to anything. Her strange drawings never seemed to fit the
assignment given by her professors. Margy spent her time adding and
dropping courses cafeteria-style. In her first two years, Margy did not
have a single positive experience; she did just enough to get by going
on and off probation with regularity.

This then was the Margy who signed up with me to study
Advanced Painting and Individual Problems last fall. I.P. is a one-on-
one situation that the student requests, and he or she is required to write
a proposal that must be approved by the instructor. It is generally
considered an independent study, and only those students who
demonstrate capability for independent study are approved. So
Margy had heard about a research grant that I had received to explore
color Xerox as an art medium and she wrote a proposal that vaguely
alluded to the possibility of combining writing with xerox imagery.
Margy found her niche, her medium, and with this the transformation
began, not only in her work, but in her attitude. She became active on
the Student Advisory Committee, she organized the annual student
exhibition, and began to show a real concern for matters bearing on

W. Martin (Ed.). *New Directions for Teaching and Learning: New Perspectives on Teaching and Learning*, no. 7.
San Francisco: Jossey-Bass, September 1981

the quality of her Carnegie-Mellon University experience.

During the spring semester Margy continued to critique the university. Her remarks were hostile: "Why doesn't this university care about its students?" Or she would take on the city: "Pittsburgh is the pits!" Her fellow students were on the receiving end: "Boy if I hear one more 'ya know'—these students sure are stupid!" Now Margy had not revealed her "problem," I had not seen the "book," the results were not in yet, not even a progress report, but something was happening to Margy. Her neglected studio, which was almost always in complete disarray, began to look neater—there was still clutter, but the clutter was the result of some serious activity. Her strange drawings began to relate to some very structured assemblage pieces that were remotely related to Russian Constructivism: Tatlin's Tower appeared on the wall of her cubicle along with photographs of Malevich and the American, Frank Stella. Still not giving in, "C-MU sucks!" was also there. Well, Margy was keeping up a front, but she was making progress. Anarchy was replaced by a quiet resolve to make her work better; our critiques became productive because we had something to discuss. Eccentricity took on a new shape with some lovely constructions. Margy was getting down to work.

I commented and she replied: "I am still a degenerate, I would rather sleep through all of this." Still no color Xerox. The last week of classes, Margy's mother was in town and I was invited to meet her. When the time came for me to say goodbye until the fall, Margy said, "Oh by the way, I have a copy of my book for you. I want to give it to you before I leave." The book is amazing; the story reveals a great deal about Margy. Was the medium the message? Was the technology the catalyst? It was never part of our studio critiques, never part of the discussion. It is not until you read the contents of the "book" that you can tell there was a connection between her independent study and her studio progress. It was an intriguing and a very positive teaching experience for me. And Margy is looking forward to her senior year, which is more than anyone would have predicted.

*Bruce Breland is a professor in the Department of Art
at Carnegie-Mellon University, Pittsburgh, Pennsylvania.*

A sense of purpose often explains a student's poor
performance and a faculty member's frustration.

Giving a Student
a Sense of Purpose

Anonymous

Jane was my freshman advisee all year, though enrolled in my Arts and
Science course only for spring term when we got to know each other
first-hand in the classroom. I had observed earlier in the year that she
had trouble completing work for my colleagues and suffered the
consequences in her grades. On several occasions, we had long,
sometimes emotional talks. She shared her feelings about procrastina-
tion and revealed what struck me as almost an addiction to a cycle of
social life that disrupted normal studies. At the end of winter, she was
on academic probation. So I was curious to see what would happen
when she finally arrived in my course.

   She spoke up in class with gusto (the course dealt with
Platonism and St. Augustine—difficult, if not rarefied material for
freshmen), though was almost always ill prepared and offered
observations that were off the wall. In my course, she completed only
one of three papers (with a "C") and did not turn in the final exam. On
the last day of the term, when it became likely that she was not going to
complete the work, I counseled her quite directly and asked in various
ways what she really hoped for in college. It was clear to me that she had
never given this question the least thought. I could never find out that

W. Martin (Ed.). *New Directions for Teaching and Learning: New Perspectives on Teaching and Learning,* no. 7.
San Francisco: Jossey-Bass, September 1981

she had even a clue about the aim of being at the college. Yet she is bright, energetic, attractive, socially at ease, athletic, and writes well.

I decided that having a purpose for one's studies is even more important than I had imagined. Some idea, even if trite, must connect the mind with the emotions and thus yield some level of satisfaction. Two weeks into the summer, after I turned in a grade of "F" to the registrar, Jane sent me an unsolicited special delivery package with all the work left undone for the term. It was skimpy at best, though possibly a low pass if turned in on time. She sent along a plea that the work be accepted so she could return to the college in the fall. I declined to accept the work. I had announced early in the class and repeated on the syllabus that late work (after the last day of classes) was not acceptable. I felt that her drifting, mindless approach to her education had gone on all year and that the only remedy was time off to think about what she wants from her education. The frustrating part of this, I think, was my utter inability to give her the sense of purpose she needs to discover for herself. No latitude or second-hand advice about education being a key to the good life would do the trick. What she needs, I reasoned, is something concrete and no one else could give it to her.

This contributor asked to remain anonymous.

A good teacher must be a good scholar.

A Teacher's Commentary:
The Desire to Be Whole Again

Harriet W. Sheridan

Good teachers believe in human perfectability, not original sin. They are brought into the profession by two forces, and, if they are lucky, those forces catalyze learning for their students. One imperative is the pursuit of truth. Scholars heed this command, knowing how arduous that pursuit will be, yet remaining addicted to the excitement of this quest. The second force is the desire to contribute something to the improvement of the society through the education of its citizens. Teachers struggle with the demands of social conscience, knowing that what they accomplish might make a difference in an individual life, might even make a difference in our futures. Scholars need not be good teachers; good teachers must always be scholars.

The motifs that interweave themselves in these teachers' essays exhibit the teacher's desire to understand students, to participate with them in the experience of learning, and to lead them to a role that transcends self-interest and enlarges into the improvement of society. For these teachers, the parable of the prodigal son, the reclaiming to a happier state of those who might be presumed lost, the welcoming to the world of the intellect, the participation in humane considerations, all

W. Martin (Ed.). *New Directions for Teaching and Learning: New Perspectives on Teaching and Learning*, no. 7.
San Francisco: Jossey-Bass, September 1981

this infuses their accounts of struggles with unresponsive classes and with students intent upon just getting by.

The dilemma of the teacher is how to balance the competing claims of both scholar and teacher, of the seeker after knowledge and the guide to virtuous living. We have inherited our dilemma from the past, from the Platonic view that holds important the "training from childhood in goodness, which makes a man eagerly desirous of becoming a perfect citizen, understanding how both to rule and be ruled righteously" (*Laws,* I, 643c-644b). The Greek view passed into the Renaissance in a fusion of energetic scholarship with godly pursuits. "I call therefore a complete and generous education," said Milton, "that which fits a man to perform, justly, skillfully and magnanimously all the offices both private and public of peace and war" (*Of Education*). It lies at the heart of Newman's four essays on the idea of a university, which conclude with the observation: "The educated mind may be said to be in a certain sense religious; that is, it has what may be considered a religion of its own" that leads to the formation of an ethical character ("Knowledge and Religious Duty," *The Idea of a University*). And it is echoed by Whitehead: "We can be content with no less than the old summary of an educational ideal which has been current at any time from the dawn of our civilization. The essence of education is that it be religious . . . an education which inculcates duty and reverence" (*The Aims of Education*).

How much easier we have found it to cultivate the scholar in our students, to inculcate the various knowledges that have been painfully accumulated. Thus, our catalogues provide course after course on the content of what we know, or think we know about the world, about social groups, about the works of the human imagination, data, facts, critical analyses, interpretations, hypotheses, equations. All this crammed into four years of so many requirements, so many papers, so many grades, so many degrees.

We are, of course, not altogether successful in this undertaking. Students persist in misunderstanding. They cannot all master paradigms or recreate models. They are bored in the laboratory. Monetarist economics confuses or affronts them. They do not much care for literature, or history, or philosophy; these studies do not seem relevant. And when they refuse to take these courses, and the humanities suffer a decline, we create a commission to study modern language instruction, or the humanities in American life, we tighten our requirements, we re-establish distribution, we indict the age for illiteracy, we look outwards for the cause, even as we have learned to sail into outer space.

But it is the inner space that counts, generally uncharted and little regarded until it makes itself known pathologically, at which time we have the university psychiatrist standing by on call.

The greatest crime of the Academy is plagiarism. One of the first lessons the new teacher learns is to stand guard. I remember my initiation into the faculty association of the watchful in the first year of my teaching at a large, public, women's college in New York City. A freshman in my composition course, asked to write a descriptive essay about an event, handed in a word-for-word copy of an essay by Thurber. I read it through; it was familiar; I reached for a book; it was published. What to do? That was over thirty-five years ago, but I still feel the agony. I blamed myself; I blamed the student; I never thought to blame the system. I wish I had thought of the response adopted by one of the teachers published in this text, who took his student the next step. "What do you want me to do then? I'll show you."

What I learned from that episode and another subsequent episode in which two young women, each in a different section, turned in identical themes, a coincidence that originated in their both dating the same young man, was to particularize my writing assignments, to line them out in a way that directly involved students' ideas and opinions, and to reduce, therefore, the desperation that has led many students to dishonesty. Yet I know students will continue to plagiarize in spite of all the efforts and all the vigilance. Should I let this knowledge poison trust?

Scholarship is a lonely task. It is practiced in the silent carrels of the library, or behind the shut door of a study. It is harder for teachers at small colleges, easier for researchers on university campuses. When the scholarship comes to completion, it is published, generally to sink without a trace—every now and then, a stir, a sharp exchange of hostilities, possibly some effect in changed content or methodology in the classroom, rarely some effect on the world, though when that happens, it is profound. But learning flourishes, as plants are said to thrive when they share each other's atmosphere, in collaboration. Education ought to be the bringing up of a student "not to live alone but amongst others . . . whereby he shall be best able to execute those doings in life, which the state of his calling shall employ unto, whether *publike* abode, or *private* at home, according unto the direction of his countrie" (Richard Mulcaster, *Positions*, 1581). Yet we have become so fearful of plagiarism that the Academy actively dissuades its members from cooperative or collaborative undertakings.

We are caught between opposites: objectives and accurate factuality versus compassionate, subjective responsiveness; authority versus distributed responsibility; individual needs versus social and communal services. How can we who have lost our faith in absolute certainties in this age—even to the point of relinquishing compulsory chapel and the language requirement—mediate amongst seemingly contradictory objectives? Strange how little the society that asks so much of its teachers is willing to reward them for their difficult and essential function.

"Knowledge is not virtue," said Newman, yet we have believed since the beginning that only that knowledge that leads to virtue can expunge original sin. We worry about the inner territory, and that worry is revealed over and over again in the remarks of the teachers published here. Why are students not as avid for instruction as we are to give it? Why do we have to turn ourselves into spontaneous troupers? Why is one class lively and another inert? Why are students not open to other students' views? What do you do with the student who is satisfied with mediocrity? Why do students cheat? Why can I not hear what they are really telling me in all but words? These are teachers' questions, not scholars', and they are difficult to answer.

I remember an interview with a young woman, a junior at a rigorous academic institution, who had racked up a superlative grade-point average based upon success in an array of tough courses. She came in because she wanted to "drop out" for a while. "Why, when you've been doing so well?" "I've been working hard," she said, "and last week I thought I wouldn't do anything except get back in touch with myself. But when I looked I found there was nobody there."

The frustration of teachers arises from the knowledge that all their teaching cannot make a student fragmented by the Academy whole again. Just as it was easy for English teachers in the past to practice their profession proudly by identifying spelling errors and grammatical mistakes, while imperfect ideas and chaotic organization passed without comment, so it is easier for academics as a whole to chide students for failing to live up to regulations for lack of participation in class discussion, and for other breaches of the academic decorum. It is harder to know what goes on in their hearts and minds; we are still busily trying to find out about our own.

Over and over again we read in teachers' statements about their struggle to make knowledge virtue. We are gratified by their pleasure when learning becomes spontaneous and students are engaged. We respect their anxious desire to know when their students understand and to adopt the right method to enhance understanding. We accept their post-lapsarian acknowledgment of the fragility of success in teaching. All of us come to recognize that like writing, teaching is a subjective activity and that the subjectivity both weakens and defines the means to a noble end. We are kept honest, and so these essays show, by the judgment we see always shining at us from within our students' eyes.

Harriet W. Sheridan is Dean of the College and professor of English at Brown University, Providence, Rhode Island. She has been Dean of the Faculty, Carleton College, Northfield, Minnesota.

Through Teaching, Learning to Handle Controversial Issues

Teachers often grapple with social, political, moral,
and ethical issues in the course of their teaching careers.
This section presents some examples of this phenomenon.

Introduction

Warren Bryan Martin

The moments presented in this section show college teachers grappling with issues—social, political, moral, and ethical—that become intertwined with teaching procedures and educational principles. Some of the statements deal with politics in colleges and universities. These show how sexism and racism penetrate teaching and learning on campus. Still others point to the connection between the life of the teacher or the student and social or political conditions in the nation and the world at large. A final group of statements presents controversial solutions to complex problems, as worked out by teachers in their relationships with students. Each reader will have to decide how he or she would have handled them.

As with other sections of this book, the underlying purpose is to help teachers help students and, in the process, help themselves. One related goal is to help students to think, to reason things through. Let me provide a classic example of how a skillful teacher can use a student's own thoughts and words to build up that student's critical abilities. Professor Edward Welbourne, Master of Emmanuel, was working with a student in the presence of another teacher, who gave this eye-witness account:

> The candidate wanted to read law. No, he said to Welbourne, he had never visited a law court. The nearest

W. Martin (Ed.). *New Directions for Teaching and Learning: New Perspectives on Teaching and Learning*, no. 7.
San Francisco: Jossey-Bass, September 1981

Assize Courts were in Nottingham, fifteen miles away from his village, and the trains and buses were few, inconvenient, and expensive for a poor schoolboy. Much as he would have liked to see the law in action he had had no opportunity.

Welbourne changed the subject, and then changed it again, and handed the questioning on to another member of the committee. At the end he asked the boy if he had any sporting interests or activities. It turned out that he was a keen cricketer, already playing for his village team. Welbourne bowled him a googly: "Do you ever see any first-class cricket?" He was a lively candidate, and never more animated than in his reply to this: "Oh, yes," he said, "Nottingham is only fifteen miles away and I have a racing bike" [Bambrough, 1974, p. 19].

The scale may be enlarged as much as you like and the pattern will still be the same—the pattern of reasoning and waiting for the light to dawn.

Teachers help students, and in the process help themselves. A second goal, then, as stated early in this book, is for the teacher through teaching to learn about him- or herself and his or her basic convictions about teaching.

Richard Hunt of Harvard University described at length (*New York Times,* Feb. 16, 1976) a disturbing encounter with his students' "no-fault" view of history. The experience came out of a course about Nazi Germany that he was giving to one hundred Harvard under-graduates in the 1970s. Though the students were not indifferent to Nazi oppressions, many seemed to hold "a despairingly deterministic view of the past and present." "I believe now," Hunt concluded, "my course became for some students a kind of projection screen for their own moral struggles and dilemmas." In his view, his students' reactions were part of "some trends of our time . . . toward a no-fault guilt-free society. One might say the virtues of responsible choice, paying the penalty, taking the consequences all appear at a low ebb today."

But what was heartening in an otherwise disturbing experience was Hunt's—the teacher's—resolve to perceive his obligations as teacher in a new way:

Next time I hope to stress more strongly my own belief in the contingencies, the open-endedness of history. Somehow I have got to convey the meaning of moral decisions and their relations to significant outcomes. Most important, I want to point out that single acts of individuals and strong stands of institutions at an early date do make a difference in the long run. This is my next assignment. Now I'm through teaching no-fault history.

Reference

Bambrough, R. *Conflict and the Scope of Reason.* Hull, England: University of Hull Press, 1974.

*How does a teacher deal with a minority student whose
subject of interest is not the class but racial inequality?*

Teaching "Loaded" Subjects
to Concerned Students

Magali Sarfatti Larson

I teach sociology, and within sociology I teach politically "loaded"
subjects: political sociology, sociology of development and under-
development, social stratification and class structure. When I used to
teach at San Francisco State, as well as during the one course I taught
at University of California at Berkeley, I can say that I was very
fortunate in establishing a particularly good rapport with black
students. In the California context (and in the later 1960s and early
1970s), what I had to teach seemed relevant and new to them; my
attention to their needs was well received; the fact that I am not
American was welcome.

I came to take it for granted that black students would be friendly
and supportive, and this has not been contradicted in the East except
once. The first course I taught at the University of Pennsylvania was
misannounced as a criminology course on Prisons and the Community;
in fact, I was teaching a course on Class and Inequality in Contemporary Society. One young black woman posed problems almost from
the beginning: she was not interested in the course but stayed because
of scheduling problems. She did not read, but talked constantly
about what she "thought," "felt," "knew" on any subject, especially the

W. Martin (Ed.). *New Directions for Teaching and Learning: New Perspectives on Teaching and Learning*, no. 7.
San Francisco: Jossey-Bass, September 1981

subjects dealing with racial inequality. Not only did she reject the bibliography (which she had not read), but she interpreted all that was said in her own way. When I tried to stop her, she addressed the other black students (four out of twelve), whose silent embarrassment she construed as support for her views. Her attacks on the white students were continuous and had to be stopped.

Finally a mild "showdown" between us occurred. She talked to me after class, probably fearing for her grade (her work was quite mediocre), and I asked her to come talk to me at my home. There she played with my five-month-old baby and talked with me for two and a half hours. She finally accepted that there might be differences among blacks, according to region, class, family background and that she could have taught me about Philadelphia black culture and society, while learning from the general works we were discussing.

I thought the problem resolved, even though so late in the semester. For the remaining month and a half, she "clammed up" and did for her final even more indifferent and mediocre work than for her mid-terms. (By the way, students at the University of Pennsylvania are strictly selected; minority students do not in general come from the area. This student was an exception—she had no problems of basic understanding, no problems with reading or writing, and was quite bright.) At the end of the semester, two out of the four other black students wrote me moving notes of thanks for the class. What could I have done differently?

For the purposes of the projected conference, I had ended my anecdote with a falsely naive question. The issue raised here is, I think, deeper than it seems, for it indirectly addresses all the problems inherent in the nature of our educational credentialing system. Underlying our students' attitudes toward education is the credentialing process, the "inevitable curse" which transforms most of their classes into imposition and drudgery. Sometimes I think that their tacit perception of the realities of the labor market explains at least some of their attitude toward their teacher, whom they see occupying a secure and authoritative place. The contrast between our "position" and their anxious knowledge about their own "lack of position" combines with other lines of conflict, such as that apparent in my story: the conflicts between our supposed objectivity and their beliefs, the violence that our analytical spirit does to an experience that engulfs them totally and immediately.

The authority that is given to us over the certification the students seek (while only half-believing in its effectiveness on the job market) vitiates the possibility of exchange "in the pursuit of knowledge or understanding," although it does not entirely cancel this possibility out. In the case I reported, I was indeed acting with a time lag: the 1960s and early 1970s had been a time in which utopian hopes blurred real social differences. My student, in 1975, could not accept the merging of her real (private, out-of-school) self with her classroom persona without jeopardizing her implicit strategy of defensive (and minimal) compliance. I think now that she was probably the most rebellious and the most interesting of the students I had, because of her refusal to compromise her "real" self with the compulsory credentialing process. Out of the classroom, she could talk with me and treat me as a real human being; in the classroom she could not. I should have learned from her refusal to "be taught"; I think I am beginning to learn. My attitude toward "disruptive" students is very different now, even though my way of approaching them—in private, if possible out of the school context—would be the same.

Magali Sarfatti Larson teaches in the Department of Sociology at Temple University, Philadelphia, Pennsylvania.

Awarding grades that the students "deserve" solves few of the difficulties of arriving at the "right" grades.

"A" for Effort

Lewis Foster

A black student in one of my philosophy courses soon showed himself to be personable, industrious, and eager, not only to learn but to do it well. He was both motivated and interested. What more can an instructor desire?

But it soon became apparent that he was in trouble. The trouble involved both comprehension and articulation. It also became obvious that he had not been adequately prepared for this level, and he knew it. But that did not stop him, and he sought me out after failing the first quiz. We went over it, content and form. I had him rewrite it. He did and it was unsatisfactory. We worked over the ideas again and his expression of them. Another rewrite. This one was better but still bad. And so on, through the semester. Now the important point is that he kept at it and always in a courteous, enthusiastic manner. Moreover, since he was naturally bright, he improved and he improved to the point where his thought was coherent and his writing clear. In fact, he had gone from "wretched" to "average," from "F" to "C."

The course work completed, I had to submit a grade for this student. But what grade? It had to be a "C" by any standard that would reflect justice to his classmates. But I submitted a "B." Why? This student showed outstanding courage, perseverance, energy, and eagerness, and he showed himself to be a gentleman, if I may use an

W. Martin (Ed.). *New Directions for Teaching and Learning: New Perspectives on Teaching and Learning*, no. 7.
San Francisco: Jossey-Bass, September 1981

outmoded term. But I never before had determined grades based on effort, only on actual academic performance. Why at this time? Well, maybe because he had worked so hard and because his skin was black.

To this day, I am not sure whether or not I did right. I am not even sure whether it was a teaching or a learning experience and for whom. I am sure that there is some kind of problem inherent in all this without knowing precisely what it is.

Lewis Foster is professor of philosophy in the Department of Philosophy at the College of William and Mary, Williamsburg, Virginia.

The question of remedial work for the poorly prepared student is a personal as well as professional question for the sensitive teacher.

Debra: A Case Study in Counseling

Anonymous

Debra is a young black woman newly recruited to attend an institution where I was in the midst of my second year as an instructor. Her ethnic identity is important to note because it affected the situation to be discussed. The institution could be classified as one of the "better" colleges. These students had relatively high academic qualifications—a large percentage had attended private schools. The percentage of Ph.D.s on the faculty was also particularly high.

There was only one minority faculty member (myself) and only one minority administrator (the black student adviser). It was part of my written and unwritten responsibility to counsel and in some cases to tutor minority students. I worked as a counselor, instructor, and tutor with Debra.

I remember seeing Debra arrive on campus. She was very shy and seemed terribly intimidated by what must have been a different and in some ways foreign environment. Debra was admitted as a "high-risk" student. Her academic performance in high school had been fair at best. She had rated in the lower half of her class. Compared with the preparation of the students that she would be competing against, her potential for matriculation was not considered very probable.

W. Martin (Ed.). *New Directions for Teaching and Learning: New Perspectives on Teaching and Learning,* no. 7. San Francisco: Jossey-Bass, September 1981

I first met Debra at the end of the first semester. Her name had been brought to my attention by faculty with whom she had taken courses. Debra had begun her freshman year taking three courses—one less than the average load taken by incoming freshmen. She received a "D" in one, an "incomplete" in another, and an "F" in the third. The three faculty got together with her adviser and agreed that her academic preparation and performance was too weak and advised that she be dismissed.

I called Debra into my office for a conference. This was the first time that I talked to her formally. Just as I began to talk to her about her academic situation, she burst into tears and continued sobbing for the next few minutes. I had received reports from her instructors that she had done this on other occasions, particularly when asked questions in class. After having reviewed her file and grade report and feeling some degree of pessimism about the prospects for continuing, I must admit that at this point, I did not think that college, or at least this particular college, was the place for her to be. I thought that the college was a very "high-risk" place for her because it affected her so much emotionally.

After a few minutes, Debra calmed down and we began to discuss her situation. Like many students from her background and unlike the larger percentage of the student body, she came from a background where there was no tradition of attending college. This was a totally new experience for her, which frightened her to a degree that few could comprehend. I did not bother to ask her about the qualifications but instead asked a very direct question. I asked if she was sincerely interested in pursuing an academic degree and if she felt she could handle the challenges and frustrations that would continue to be a part of this experience. Painfully aware of her academic deficiencies, she responded that she knew that she would have to do a lot of growing up and that, nonetheless, she still wanted to continue pursuing her education where she was. She viewed her problem as one of adjustment, and she also felt that her instructors did very little to accommodate her adjustment. She felt that they did little more than acknowledge her presence.

I discussed her situation with the black student adviser and with each of the three faculty. The black student adviser and I, perhaps because we had had similar experiences, felt that she should be given a second chance. On the other hand, each of the other three faculty had given up hope for her. Nonetheless, Debra was given a second chance and after much growth and development and to everyone's astonishment, she eventually graduated from the college four and one-half years later. The point that I wish to emphasize is only indirectly related to Debra. The awareness brought about as a result of her situation (and there were many others with similar problems in the minority and nonminority student population) led to the convening of a conference that consisted of faculty, administrators, and staff working in the special services (tutoring) area. The debate was what was the college's commitment to students in need of remedial work.

Many issues were raised and addressed at this meeting, which at times got very emotional. After the meeting had progressed for some time, certain philosophical points of view rose to the surface. There seemed to be a consensus that the college would be compromising too much in both resources and reputation by bringing in students in need of remedial services. What disturbed me the most was hearing some of the professors use terminology such as "ignorant" and "boneheads" in referring to these students. To be fair, it is important to note that there were others on the faculty who were sensitive to Debra's special needs and who obviously supported her as she progressed through the years. A small percentage of the faculty urged further support for the special services program in part as a result of the conference. However, the outcome of the conference did not produce any significant changes. The institution's commitment to the special services area was not expanded as I felt it should have been, but instead was slightly retrenched.

The entire experience was instructive for many reasons. The most important lesson I learned was never to give up on anyone who has the will and determination to give his or her best efforts. I could relate to Debra's personal struggle because I had experienced many parallel situations within my own educational career. At the same time, something within me made me question whether or not it was appropriate to recruit students who have needs that an institution is not committed to meet adequately. I became very suspicious of the institutional motivations for recruiting such students. The final consideration is a philosophical one that addresses itself to the wider question of where faculty and institutions place their emphasis in terms of time and resources in meeting the needs of students and, by extension, the larger society. Is it more important to spend the larger percentage of time and money to help the "high achiever" — as is the emphasis of the faculty just mentioned? Or, as I believe, is it better to concentrate on those who need the special services remedial work and one-on-one assistance to make the most of their educational experience? This is a basic philosophical question that everyone in the realm of teaching and learning is confronted with at one time or another.

This contributor asked to remain anonymous.

*A teacher risks serious misunderstanding by refusing
to accept racial stereotyping as an excuse for poor academic
performance.*

Have You Ever Taught Before?

Miriam Stamps

The first year that I taught, I decided to give an essay exam in my
freshman Introduction to Business course. The students were not
pleased because they had only had to write essays for their English
courses and had always taken true-false or multiple choice exams in
their other classes. They were even less pleased when the papers were
returned and they received very poor grades.

When I asked the class what the problem seemed to be, they
asked me if I had ever taught before. I told them I had, and they then
asked if my previous students had been white. When I told them that
they had been white, their response was "Well, you can't expect us to
be able to write like they did because we are black."

This remark thoroughly incensed me and I told them so. I told
them that I would not accept blackness as an excuse for mediocrity,
and that their comment would have caused a riot if it had been spoken
by a white person. I told them that if their excuse was they they had not
been exposed to essay writing and therefore did it poorly, I could
accept that as a reason for their poor performance, and that we could
work toward solving the problem. I suppose the reason that I was so
upset was that these students has been told for so long that they were
inferior that they had internalized this feeling and were now willing and
eager to use this as an excuse without seeking ways to overcome
whatever weaknesses they may have had.

W. Martin (Ed.). *New Directions for Teaching and Learning: New Perspectives on Teaching and Learning*, no. 7.
San Francisco: Jossey-Bass, September 1981

Miriam Stamps an assistant professor at Lemoyne College, Syracuse, New York.

*A student's excuses for not getting work done can be
justifiable ones, and a teacher may experience great reward
in permitting a student a second chance.*

A Second Chance

Silvia T. Zsoldos

Our university offers a five-week "winterim" semester. Originally designed for experimental work, the winterim now also schedules many regular courses, but in the pressure-cooker situation of twenty-five class meetings, each lasting one and one-half hours. With the time constraints, students cannot afford to miss many of the daily meetings and must keep up with their reading assignments.

During the last winterim, I taught the second half of a United States history survey course to a large section. One of the students, Ann, a quiet, pale slip of a girl was a declared history major. She missed her first mid-term examination and came to see me about a make-up examination. She had been ill and had had some personal problems also. I agreed to the make-up, she took it, and did not do particularly well. I was a bit surprised, for in our conference she had seemed to have a grasp of the subject matter, but before I could give the examination back to her, she missed three days of classes. Her roommate finally came in to explain that Ann was in the infirmary, having injured her knee by slipping on ice on her way to class. A classmate, however, was supplying her with the daily lecture notes. Ann came to class for a day, then missed two more, and her roommate showed up to explain that Ann had, again, slipped on the ice while trying to maneuver on her crutches. I verified the story from the infirmary.

W. Martin (Ed.). *New Directions for Teaching and Learning: New Perspectives on Teaching and Learning*, no. 7.
San Francisco: Jossey-Bass, September 1981

Eventually, Ann came for a conference. She explained her first mid-term—that she had not slept because of personal problems but that she had now pulled herself together. She knew she had missed a lot and needed my permission to go on with the course. I pointed out, as gently as I could, that she had made a poor showing for a major in her first exam, that she had missed many lectures, that if her second mid-term was not a good one she stood to lose a lot. I suggested that she could drop the course without penalty in light of her injuries so that she could take it again in the spring semester. The drop-add period was over, but I was sure I could help her work it out.

Ann was upset. She explained that she is normally a good student and that she would work very hard. She needed the course now as a prerequisite for her spring work and asked that I let her try anyway. I was worried that she might really get hurt and lose her self-confidence but agreed to go along with her request and to work with her if she came to the review sessions I held in my office. Since I do have an announced policy of regarding the first mid-term examination as the least important in assigning the final grade, Ann did have a chance, although a small one.

Ann's second mid-term went well. Thereafter she missed no more classes and worked demonstrably hard, producing a solid "A" for her final examination. She could now go on to her next course assignments, and I felt good about the outcome.

A couple of months later, Ann hailed me in the corridor. She wanted to thank me for having given her the chance to try, even though the odds were against her. She admitted candidly that my doubts had hurt her but said that she had realized later that, in the circumstances, I could not have offered her great encouragement. The main point, for which she would remember me, was that I had not shut the door but had left it open for her to go on. I felt "like a million dollars" the rest of the day.

The last time I saw Ann was in the department's office where she was looking for her adviser to plan her fall schedule. I remembered and resolved again that my job as a teacher is to open and to hold open the doors to education, even against odds, for I can never tell ahead of time who will be able to go through them.

Silvia T. Zsoldos is a lecturer at the University of Delaware, Newark, Delaware.

A teacher ponders what is "enough" in the way of trying to help a student get over a difficult hurdle.

A Third Chance

Judith Stitzel

It was not until she was ready to take her master's exam for the third time that I began to wonder whether it had been strange that I had not made it my business to read the two previous examinations that she had failed. I was not her official adviser. She had at first intended to do a creative writing thesis, and though I read and commented on all her writing, I was not an official member of the creative writing segment of the department and could not officially advise her.

The first time she took her exam, she took it, as she said, as a trial run. So when she failed it, neither one of us was very upset. The second time she failed it, almost a year later, she said she had studied very hard, and felt she understood the material, and attributed her failure at least in part to an error in the way in which the exam was presented (historical periods supposed to be on the second day's exam were, in fact, on the first day's)—an error that the department administration acknowledged but that it did not feel was serious enough to invalidate the results of the exam and that no student complained about officially.

When she told me she had failed the exam a second time, she seemed very calm about it, and I think now that in my relief at her apparent calm, I failed to register some other responses, such as the anger that the calm was masking. I told her that I was very sorry, that if

W. Martin (Ed.). *New Directions for Teaching and Learning: New Perspectives on Teaching and Learning,* no. 7.
San Francisco: Jossey-Bass, September 1981

there was anything I could do, I would be glad to, that I would be happy to go over the exam with her if she wanted to bring it to me after she had gone over it, that I would be happy to write out study questions for her. She thanked me and asked for nothing.

I did not go and look at her exam. One of the reasons was that because of my affection for her I was afraid of interfering inappropriately. It was "enough" I told myself that I had offered to go over the exam if she brought it to me. And I still think that I was right about that (although the "enough" strikes me as a curious word—enough for what? for whom?). But there was another feeling that I did not let myself experience until later—I was afraid that I might agree with the examiners. She had never officially taken a class with me. All I had seen was her fiction. And her fiction had convinced me of the importance of encouraging her. She was writing a long autobiographical novel, spanning many generations. She was trying to make sense in her own life, in her own lifetime, in her own words, of terrifying events that (especially since they reflected the outsider's vision of what it was to be an Appalachian) she needed to understand and to assimilate.

Her style did not always come up to her content, to put it in the most simplistic terms. There were even some problems with grammar and punctuation and spelling. And yet none of this got in the way of my conviction that she was dealing with very important material—not just in a therapeutic sense, but as an artist, a writer, a lover of language, someone wanting to give shape to and share experience. Nonetheless, when she failed the exam a second time, some of my confidence in her, which meant (I realized later) some of my confidence in myself, had been eroded. Had I perhaps overestimated her? Was I pampering her? Was I being too soft?

Although my students' evaluations do not reflect this, I believe that I have a reputation among some of my colleagues for being soft, for indulging students. I do not think this is true, and yet I worry about it. It is true that over the years many of the students who have worked with me have needed some additional help in one way or another. It is true that I get involved in the emotional as well as the intellectual life of my students. It is what my students (and even some of my colleagues) appreciate. And yet, in times of stress, it does give me trouble. This was a time of stress.

When three weeks before she was to retake her exam for the third (and probably last time) she came to see me, for the first time visibly upset, she told me that she had been trying all semester to had asked them several times and that when they finally did see her, she got conflicting reports, some faculty particularly liking answers that others had singled out for criticism. She felt that the whole thing was being poorly handled and she brought up again the fact that the exam she had failed the previous time had been incorrectly administered. She was very angry. Upon my recommendation, she went to see the chairwoman of the department about her difficulty in getting to see people about the exam; the chairwoman spoke to the faculty member who had been particularly delinquent and urged a meeting. The reports of that meeting from the student and the faculty member differed, and the chairwoman, whose opinion I generally respect, found herself annoyed with the student's account. In other words, things were getting complicated.

They were further complicated by the fact that the weekend before the exam the student was planning to attend a conference (which I would also be attending) on Appalachian women writers, and this despite the fact that she had been finding it hard to concentrate on studying for the exam. I could understand her desire to attend. She was a writer; it was what she did best. At the conference she would be in touch with the part of herself that was succeeding. She would get some reinforcement she sorely needed. And yet I felt myself wanting to tell her that she should not go, that she should stay home and study, give it her best shot. I agonized over whether to interfere. I was very self-conscious about the possible accusation that I was mothering her (even though I had recently heard Tillie Olsen speak eloquently about the appropriateness of our mothering our students if we understand "mothering" correctly). I was also uncomfortable having to admit to myself that a good chunk of the reason I wanted her not to go was not for her but for me. If she took the exam again and failed, I knew that in some way or another, I would be heavily involved in what followed. If it came to fighting for her, I knew I would not be able to do it in the face of the accusation "and she didn't even spend the last weekend studying!"

I finally decided to call her and to tell her I thought it would be a good idea for her to stay home and study. I told her I would understand either decision but that I would be much more comfortable with her staying home. I told her that if she went and failed, it would be debilitating always to be wondering whether she would have passed "if. . . ." I know it is hard to believe, but I cannot remember whether I told her straight out that if she went to the conference and failed the exam, it would make things difficult for me. I know I did not tell her about the doubts about my own competence that made me doubt hers.

She decided to stay home. She passed the exam. I have no idea to what extent the two events are related. I know I was grateful— very grateful— for both.

Judith Stitzel is a professor in the Department of English at West Virginia University, Morgantown.

Modifying the conduct of a course involves not only an
attempt to understand students but to reach a better
understanding of oneself.

Dealing with Students Who Are "Turned Off"

Roland Haynes

I began working at the University of South Carolina during a time of drastic social change. My instructional assignment consisted of teaching two lower-division courses and one upper-division course. The majority of my class members were freshmen. Some upper-class and graduate students comprised a fairly good mixture. Most of these students came from the South. Other students were from the North and Northeast. This made for an interesting variety. The majority of the students attending my class, Psychology of Adjustment, consisted of non-psychology majors. Most of them were taking a psychology course for the first time with the exception of those who had been exposed to a course in high school.

    The class met in an extremely large room. We called it the inner sanctum because when one walked across the floor it squeaked like the floor of the classic haunted house. The hidden agenda for most students was "how to make it" in the course. "Making it" meant simply how to succeed in making an "A" without really trying. I struggled, becoming more aware I would be teaching students who were enrolled in the course, and not merely teaching the course, that was a hard one to master, since so many of the variables were built into

W. Martin (Ed.). *New Directions for Teaching and Learning: New Perspectives on Teaching and Learning*, no. 7.
San Francisco: Jossey-Bass, September 1981

the experience, which some described as a sure waste of time. Involvement in the discipline of day-by-day experiences would support or reject this hypothesis.

At the outset, most students who attended seemed to respond favorably to the presentation of my syllabus and an overall projection of what the course would be like. I did notice, through conversations, movement of chairs, and the like, that a handful of students seemed turned off. I wondered if that kind of behavior would represent the "shape of things to come." After the class, I attempted to revise my schedule and syllabus in order to anticipate basic learning and teaching needs of myself and my students. I thought of the somewhat authoritarian means of asking those students who seemed to be turned off for whatever reason to see me after class in my office. I quickly dismissed the idea, realizing it would further intimidate perhaps all of the students in the class. Instead, I approached the class with a suggestion box idea since it fitted the student-centered format that seemed quite popular in those days. A few students wrote suggestions about how they would like to see the class proceed from this point on. After reading the suggestions, I became more aware of the importance of such a step. I also tried to help the class put these ideas into effect with the continuation of the next class session. However, there was still the small group that remained talkative during lectures and group presentations. I reviewed one expert's views. His sound strategy for developing effective discussion in teaching consisted of the need to "(1) use the resources of members of the group; (2) give students opportunities to formulate applications of principles; (3) help students learn to think in terms of the subject matter by giving them practice in thinking; (4) help students learn to evaluate the logic of, and evidence for, their own and others' positions; (5) help students become aware of and formulate problems using information to be gained from readings or lectures; (6) gain acceptance for information or theories counter to folklore or previous beliefs of students; and (7) develop motivation for further learning" (McKeachie, 1978).

At the midsemester mark, a young man came to my office one afternoon. He introduced himself. I invited him to take a seat and recognized him to be one of my students in Psychology of Adjustment. He immediately expressed guilt and regret for having been one of the students who had caused noise and distractions during the class. His demeanor was one of honesty and the long overdue need for release concerning the subject. He mentioned some undercurrent of feeling that existed in the class. He felt some of the feeling was justified. He also added he did not feel the manner in which his friends were registering their complaints was fair. I struggled to be honest. I tried during this visit to set the stage for more open discussion and listen carefully to him without displacing his agenda with mine because of ego or pride. From my conversation with him, I realized the need to modify some learning objectives and methods originally planned in connection with the course.

After midsemester, members of the original core of distractors who were dissatisfied with the course dropped by my office to see me. Sometimes they came individually and then in a group. Gradually a steady stream of students visited with me as the weeks passed. The class helped me to take a good look at myself, my role, and my goals as teacher. Emerging from this intensive period of introspection was the formation of a new syllabus.

As the second semester started, I opened the class with that new syllabus. From my new insights, I tried harder to earn from my students their commitment to study with me. I remembered that the grades of the small group of dissatisfied students of the first semester's class had radically improved: some had risen from "D's" to "B's" and others from "C's" to "A's."

I learned much from this class. Most of all, I learned more about myself.

Reference

McKeachie, W. *Teaching Tips: a Guidebook for the Beginning College Teacher.* Lexington, Mass.: Heath, 1978.

Roland Haynes is an associate professor in he Department of Psychology, at the University of South Carolina, Columbia.

Sometimes "messy human affairs" will take precedence over a strict adherence to academic standards.

A Generous Solution to a Sticky Problem

Janice Kemp

As a teacher, I have always had difficulty placing myself on the continuum between being unyielding, demanding, and authoritarian and being a softhearted easy mark for students who have learned to "work the system." Although I did not always appreciate "tough" professors at the time, I have come to respect the knowledge and discipline their approach engendered. This is perhaps one reason why I tend to adopt a relatively hard-line approach to problem situations. This approach is tempered by one experience in which a professor "bent" his rules for me.

One semester I overextended myself almost to the point of nervous collapse. I was to receive my B.A. in the middle of my fourth year in college. Although I only needed fifteen hours to graduate, I took an additional course because I had always been interested in the subject and because the professor was reputed to be particularly inspiring. This course load was made heavier by the drain on my time of a position as a dormitory counselor, which provided room and board. Further complicating the semester was a decision to marry. Since my family would be traveling several hundred miles to attend

W. Martin (Ed.). *New Directions for Teaching and Learning: New Perspectives on Teaching and Learning,* no. 7. San Francisco: Jossey-Bass, September 1981

my graduation, my fiancé and I decided to schedule the ceremony for the same weekend, making their trip doubly worthwhile.

The course work was particularly demanding that semester. Several papers were due in the last three weeks. The harder I worked at the papers, lab research projects, studying for exams, making wedding plans, and working in the dorm, the more there seemed to be left to do before the rapidly advancing deadline of finals week. Somehow I managed to do everything but finish the paper for that "extra" course. The outline was completed, but I could not write. Every time I sat to write the other pressures flooded into my consciousness and the paper remained blank. What was to happen? I could not write. Without the paper I could not complete the course. I could not graduate with an incomplete. My registration as a graduate student the next week depended on receiving the B.A. The position as a graduate assistant that was to put food on the table would be jeopardized if I could not register as a graduate student. It looked as if the war would be lost for want of a nail. As finals week ended and the paper still had not miraculously materialized, I went to the professor to tearfully explain the situation. At some point in the lengthy interview, the discourse turned to the content of the would-be paper—what I had read, the outline, what I would have written if only I could. The professor made the most humane decision possible. He suggested that our conversation serve as an equivalent to writing the paper.

At times, when faced with similar decisions as a teacher, I have wondered what were, for him, the critical elements of the situation that led to his decision. Surely there are times when students must face the consequences of their choices and actions. Maintaining standards of academic excellence is a primary function of the professor. Alternately there are times when strict adherence to "standards" serves to stifle rather than promote human growth, which is what education is supposed to be all about. Is not the unswerving maintenance of "standards" by some, in reality, merely an ivory tower mechanism to avoid muddying the waters of academia with messy human affairs? If one takes a more situational approach, at what point does humanitarianism become irresponsibility to the profession? Determining this point is sometimes difficult, and I find the judgment seat uncomfortable.

Janice Kemp is an instructor in Biology at Central College, Pella, Iowa.

*The joy of genuine learning is too often lost in the
competitive atmosphere of university work.*

A Member of the Dance

Mary Wilson Carpenter

Recently I watched a performance by the Paul Taylor Dance Company—
a consummately beautiful performance that practically lifted me out of
my seat. I experienced that special kind of pleasure in superb art that is
closer to a feeling of joy than to esthetic delight. And I remembered
how I had come by the capacity for that kind of response in watching
dancers. As a child, I attended a camp where you signed up for one
particular activity all morning every morning, and I had chosen the
dance unit my first summer there. As it turned out, I was a lousy
dancer, so I spent more of my time watching other kids practice their
acts than dancing myself. You might think this was an unhappy
experience, but it was not—far from it. Instead, I learned how to
perceive—how to observe and to feel—the attempts of others to
master their art. I learned to distinguish the technically perfect but
emotionally flat movement from the aspiring movement where, even
though the dancer slipped, the reach and the desire toward some new
peak made the watcher's heart pound.

My experience in many graduate seminars has seemed much
the same: there has been a joy in watching other students stretch to do
the best work they have ever done—a special joy in sensing the aspira-
tion, the best-yet, of papers that were admittedly full of flaws, incomplete, even amateurish. Perhaps I was lucky I had several teachers who

W. Martin (Ed.). *New Directions for Teaching and Learning: New Perspectives on Teaching and Learning,* no. 7.
San Francisco: Jossey-Bass, September 1981

seemed able to share in, or even to create, that sense of joy in the dance, of mutual striving for perfection and of genuinely mutual joy when a fellow "dancer" managed something good, something aspiring.

My problem is that the teaching world does not seem to be like that. I have already seen too many instances in which one teacher tried to discredit the beautiful performance of another, strictly out of a fear of competition. This is not the same as fair criticism: it is pure egotism. I am aware that the academic profession has never been without it, and I am also aware that my complaint may seem either holier-than-thou or naive, or both. My problem is that I do not want to lose that capacity for joy in a fellow dancer's aspiring motion. How can I, first of all, fend off the green-eyed monsters of professional jealousies and anxieties? What kinds of attitudes and values, professional habits and practices, distinguish the teacher who is at least relatively free of such plagues? And second, how can I promote a spirit of mutual striving among my own students, of delight in someone else's achievement while each individual yet feels encouraged to see his or her own peak? I am speaking of the attempt to instill—and to experience in myself—a spirit of community.

Mary Wilson Carpenter is a teaching assistant and a Newcombe Fellow at Brown University, Providence, Rhode Island.

The basic question of how to combine being a teacher-scholar with being a person leads to other questions about how one meets the obligations teaching and living entail.

Professional Trade-Offs

Lois Hinckley

In my seventh year of college teaching, I wrote to a very senior professor I had met and had a good talk with, feeling we were in some way kindred spirits. I explained to her in the letter that the reason I wanted to pursue the acquaintance was that she struck me as a person who has successfully managed to combine being a teacher-scholar and a person, and that I would like to learn how to do the same in my own career. She wrote back, in a quite friendly fashion, but with genuine surprise that I should feel there is any discrepancy between the two or three roles. And, indeed, by her account, I feel I must have been mistaken.

Teaching, she wrote, is a very personal affair in which people study people and their societies (we are both in classics) in company with other persons. The literature, philosophy, and history of previous times may also suggest ways we can improve our own lives and those of our students. However shaped by accepted methodologies, one's perceptions of the material will also be particularly one's own; no two teachers or scholars ever read a play exactly the same way. Research, too, is involved with persons, and its goal, publication of one's work, is a kind of teaching extended over space and time.

Her account sounds so natural and right that I tried it on in my

W. Martin (Ed.). *New Directions for Teaching and Learning: New Perspectives on Teaching and Learning*, no. 7. San Francisco: Jossey-Bass, September 1981

mind, like a piece of clothing, seeing where it pinched or hung loose, where the "but's" occurred, and wondering why my frame is shaped differently, if it is.

Some of the "but's" clearly come from personal experiences. First, teacher-scholar versus person. Her account sounds inspiring but rather an overwhelming task. I realize that to me "being a person" means largely having an "off-duty" life, with its own activities and associates—what one does after going home and kicking off the shoes. Because I never saw my teachers or, for that matter, my parents in their "off-duty" times, I assumed they never wanted or made room for such times. My ex-husband, as another example, regarded himself as an extremely dedicated scholar, looked down on most of the other students as uncommitted, and could never commit himself in advance to taking time off. From these experiences, I got the message: "Committed teachers/scholars or responsible adults do not get time off." On the other hand, I suspect this is a more general problem as well. In the process of instilling responsibility and self-discipline in their children, many parents forget to remind them to retain the child's capacity and need for "nothing" time. The notion that "life is real and life is earnest" may be taken too far. A second "but"—scholar versus teacher–counselor—may be a similar mix of personal and general experience. It is all very well, I reply to my senior colleague, to show how involved with persons teaching is, but how should I allot my time between the persons requiring assistance of different kinds right now and those more distant beneficiaries, readers of my publications or next weeks's students whose material I should now be preparing? Isn't Susan in my office, obviously upset and discouraged about her freshman year as a whole, more important than the idea for an article that may not pan out or than footnote thirty-five? In any case, publishing is seldom urged on junior faculty from any such high-minded educational motives as benefiting others: instead we are warned "publish or perish," an impulse of pure self-preservation that sounds about as attractive to some of us as "winning by intimidation." Wasn't I hired to teach? Shouldn't I therefore spend my summers preparing courses so as to teach better? In my own case, since counseling is a strength, I tried living in a dorm for two years, where 440 undergraduates provide almost unlimited opportunities for being variously useful—to the point where, having overdosed, I learn that I cannot survive without some time alone both to write and think and simply to be. (I still feel that I should be able to do without these.) Again, one never sees one's role models in the process of recuperating!

The third and fourth "but's" are more clearly products of social changes. The kind of dedicated teacher-scholar my senior colleague describes perhaps originated when each such individual had a wife-figure to complement his activities and priorities. Nowadays, many of our spouses are also dedicated to something, and many of us are trying to embody in our single selves both the dedicated professional and the complementary figure who takes care of daily life. How can I combine the Big Three (Teacher-Scholar-Person) with (1) household and physical maintenance (cooking, bills, exercise, laundry—let alone children); (2) other skills I might wish to acquire (playing music, writing poetry); and (3) other people, such as relatives, on whom I may both wish and have to spend time? How much and how many of these will I have to surrender as a single professional? How much will their surrender diminish my understanding and communication abilities for the literature I teach, which was, after all, as my colleague points out, written by persons about persons for persons?

My fourth "but" is something I must contend with as a woman. Traditional assumptions about women's roles and excellences make it hard to be professional and personal at the same time. I have sometimes found that my caring for students' whole college experience and their personal as well as academic growth makes me suspect to my colleagues as being "maternal," though I never hear "paternal" used to describe even sensitive and caring male colleagues. Departmental appreciation for these activities is always ex post facto. My caring attitude also makes people assume that I must be easily gullible, an easy grader, and one who sets too low standards. My presentations of the literature as relevant to life, I feel, would be less suspect if they came from a male, who would not be so often assumed to be valuing intuition over reasoning. I am not willing to pretend to be as tough or as cool or as cynical as the male stereotype, yet I want my ideas to be judged without reference to the sex of the author. These are some of the considerations I will be putting to my senior colleague. I have drawn the "but's" rather starkly for clarity's sake; I am aware of more shadings of gray than I mention here. I do not know my senior colleague well enough to know what her trade-offs have been (she was married to another professor, now dead; they had no children), but I am hopeful, because she has at least kept the warmth along with the professionalism. I am less encouraged by others in my field, though, who seem to have lost their flexibility, self-humor, perspective, or kindliness—in short, their humanity—along the way. I suspect there is no "answer," but I could learn a good deal from other people's experiences, solutions, and compromises. I know at least that I need more varied "models."

Lois Hinckley is an associate professor in the Department of Classics at West Virginia University, Morgantown.

In suspecting a student of trying to con her,
a teacher gets a first lesson in academic politics.

Teacher, Scholar, Politician

Delores Williams

1:30 A.M. The phone rings, My voice fumbles out of a bad dream into the telephone growling "hello!" A masculine voice on the other end, "Ms. Williams, I won't be in class tomorrow. My aunt has died suddenly, and I have to go to Chicago." (Damnit, I say to myself, why call me in the middle of the night?) "Ok," I hear myself say calmly, "I'm sorry your aunt died. I'll give you the assignments when you return." He continues: "I feel I ought to stay in Chicago a few days to console my mother; it was her only sister. So I won't be able to turn in my mid-term exam for another two weeks." I swallow hard trying to conceal my anger at what looks like a put-on. I'm a new teaching assistant and do not want the rep of being a pushover for con games. Anyway, this student challenges everything I do in class; he misses whenever he feels like it; he does not do very good work. "Mr. Smith, it is unfortunate your aunt died," I say, "but I will not accept your exam later than due date. You have had plenty of time to prepare it." He gently pleads. Finally he gets angry at my resistance and hangs up the phone screaming he is going to get satisfaction.

Next day he goes to the professor, who supports me. Later, he goes to the dean, who supports him. The rationale for the dean's action is communicated to me by the professor. But I am mad as a wet hen because I feel the dean has bought a con game. My friends advise

W. Martin (Ed.). *New Directions for Teaching and Learning: New Perspectives on Teaching and Learning*, no. 7.
San Francisco: Jossey-Bass, September 1981.

me not to make waves because of my lowly situation (a student) and the politics of graduate school programs. Hence I do not complain. Rather, I learn an important lesson: the teacher-scholar must also become aware of the politics that govern relationships, create situations, and help determine promotions at an academic institution. Teacher-scholar-politician: how does one balance these roles (or merge them) when one regards teaching a calling and seeks satisfaction from a life of college teaching?

Delores Williams is a research associate at the Harvard Divinity School, Cambridge, Massachusetts.

*Faculty self-interest in the graduate school
gives a prospective teacher second thoughts
about entering the teaching profession.*

Cooperation and Competition

Marina Roseman

I came to graduate school expecting professionalism from my professors. I thought to find an enlightened humanism among the faculty, due to their advanced education. I looked forward to joining a group of people dedicated to advancing the state of knowledge and social life in their academic field and the world. Instead, I found an atmosphere of competitive suspicion in which brilliant and innovative junior faculty members were considered threatening by their senior faculty. Three times at three graduate institutions, I saw young, excellent women faculty denied tenure or denied promotion. All these women were provocative in classroom teaching, active on committees, presented original research at professional conferences, and had had publications accepted. In all the "official" categories of professorial evaluation, these candidates ranked as outstanding. Why, then, were they not being positively reinforced for their contributions to teaching and scholarship? Why were they dismissed rather than rehired?

Perhaps their youthful, scholarly productivity was perceived as an embarrassing contrast to many of the complacent, inactive tenured faculty. These young women whose engaging classroom techniques and newly composed lecture notes gained them dedicated student followings, were viewed as competitors rather than contributors by

W. Martin (Ed.). *New Directions for Teaching and Learning: New Perspectives on Teaching and Learning,* no. 7.
San Francisco: Jossey-Bass, September 1981

their colleagues. The classroom and research success of these junior faculty members, which should have been hailed as welcome additions to their fields of study, were instead met by jealousy and disapproval.

What has happened to our evaluative criteria, when the qualities of brilliance and innovation are not appreciated, but suspect? Watching this scenario repeated at three separate graduate institutions, I began to fear that "tenure" stood only for the "institutionalization of mediocrity." "Nice guys" who did not take forceful stands regarding policy changes, and whose work was passable but not necessarily innovative, gained entrance into the faculty "key club." Outspoken, creative thinkers did not.

The consequences for students were disastrous. The instability of the junior faculty's positions created a situation of constantly shifting alliances. Decisions about faculty hiring and firing—which deeply affected the students' programs—were made with slight student input and never a student vote. One's thesis adviser might be there one year and gone the next. The lack of continuity was detrimental to the students' learning processes, which unfold over years rather than merely semesters. We were denied the chance to grow in knowledge with professors who knew our work and could chart our transformations. Furthermore, we experienced intense discouragement when we saw our models—our prized instructors—debased rather than reinforced. I began to seriously question entering the educational institution as a teacher myself, for it seemed that priorities and evaluative criteria had become confused and inadequate.

The problem of faculty evaluation is crucial to the learning experience, for it directly determines faculty constituents with whom the students will be studying. And, in my opinion, it strikes to the heart of a problem that is endemic throughout academia: How are we to balance the negative pressures of an increasingly competitive job arena with the cooperative venture of furthering knowledge? And how are we to promote higher values in education if we allow our actions as faculty and department members to be corrupted by competitive self-interest?

Marina Roseman is a teacher in the Department of Anthropology, at Cornell University, Ithaca, New York.

Teachers themselves must take political power in order to empower their students so as to prepare them in turn to be politically responsible citizens.

A Teacher's Commentary: The Political Drama of Teaching

John J. MacAloon

Politics we take to be the art of exercising power fairly and judiciously for desired ends. In the classroom, general and institutional standards of quality, competence, and propriety intersect with the motives, expectations, and interests of the students, largely in the person of the teacher. The teacher's power to organize discourse and to evaluate performance is justified by his or her responsibility to adjudicate these multiple standards and aims.

Happily, their fit is often non-problemmatic, even automatic, and the teaching and learning process carries forward unperturbed. But as these statements show, just as frequently intentions and criteria are in fundamental contradiction with one another, and teachers are asked to sort through and synthesize what their society, their profession, their institution, and their students cannot or will not. Face to face with individual superiors and students, caught up in highly personal dramas of character and condition, sensitive teachers cannot do what legislators, foundation workers, professional ethics panels, deans, and college catalogue writers do: issue pious statements then break for tea.

The writer of "Debra: A Case Study in Counseling" thought an institution's purposes were served by recruiting minority students but

W. Martin (Ed.). *New Directions for Teaching and Learning: New Perspectives on Teaching and Learning*, no. 7.
San Francisco: Jossey-Bass, September 1981

not by committing the resources required by the underprepared among them. Out of caring and conviction as to the importance of their work, Judith Stitzel supervised marginal students whose official program committee and advisers couldn't be bothered. In return, she was rewarded with a reputation as an indulger of students. Lois Hinckley has suffered from this too, and knows it to be a form of sexism in the purportedly egalitarian academy. She is, moreover, torn between the two conventional images of the successful teacher/scholar that have been presented to her: one insisting on the value of taking time off to think, feel, relax, and remain a whole person; the other suggesting that no one who so indulges herself could possibly be a serious and dedicated academic. Mary Carpenter wonders how it is possible to instill mutuality, community, and a love of process among students, when egotism, competition for places, and worship of the product time to control social relations among colleagues.

One contributor notes the most obscene sacrilege within the supposed "profession"—the presence of individuals who take their mission to be the sorting out of the "boneheads" from the bright, rather than the dedicated teaching of all students. Magali Larson appears to run afoul when her discipline's assumption that because it is *about* politically loaded subjects the classroom need not *itself* be politically loaded does not square with a student's own perceptions of the situation. Together with Miriam Stamps, she struggles with the double vision of American higher education, with whether to encourage students to take themselves as representatives of particular social groups or whether to hold them to a universalistic set of standards. Lewis Foster, "for effort," bumps a minority student's grade a notch, then feels guilty. Not only has he broken his own principle of evaluating, "only on actual academic performance," but he cannot bring himself as a result of the experience to incorporate "effort" into his notion of performance and apply this new standard of merit to all students equally, in which case the problem of justice would seemingly disappear.

Foster makes a further telling remark about this episode. He is not sure "whether it was a teaching or a learning experience and for whom." As much as standards, responsibility for consequences lies at the center of the politics of teaching and connect it to the matter of politics at large. Our American notion of politics as the art of compromise in episodes of localized power is based on a view of political life as a series of discrete and self-contained situations in which time is discontinuous and actors arrive at one resolution only to begin moving all over again toward the next. The advantage of this configuration of things is that decisions do get made. Its disadvantage is that the development of insight and consensus over time is maimed, and persons may easily shrive themselves of responsibility for the long-term consequences of their action.

Our organization of teaching and learning replays this contradiction. Education is designed to be lived in spurts, bounded out in courses of determined length, foreclosed by the "resolutions" of exams and grades. After which the student passes from sight to begin again in someone else's course, then again in someone else's. In practice, the degree is, like the doings of a legislature, a series of self-contained situations. Yet we understand learning to be processual and cumulative, with respect to the development of individual students, in our design of curricula around "programs," and in our advising functions. If the political morality of teaching be understood not only as the adjudication of conflicting standards, but also as the responsibility for the consequences of our instruction upon students, where does the responsibility begin and end? "Business-like" colleagues find the limits at the classroom door and the grade report. Sensitive teachers, too, feel the pressure and the license to accept this resolution and are uneasy when they tamper with it. Yet, neither can they abandon what they know to be the real temporal and moral configuration of teaching and learning.

Foster, one senses, struggles to take faith that his grading decision will result in the student's growing competence and self-worth in successive courses. More important than his absolute authority over a single course, Roland Haynes realized, was its consequences for his future development as a teacher. He took the risk of allowing his student to help him "take a good look at himself" as a teacher and labored not to displace a student's agenda with his own "out of ego and pride." Stitzel saw that her doubts about her student's competence were mixed with doubts about her own. Rather than evading each, she faced the consequences of intervening. Miriam Stamps did not hesitate to take the heat for challenging complicated and comfortable racial stereotyping in her classroom. The anonymous teacher put his own judgment, credibility, and institutional position to the test against faculty who had given up on a student, in effect joining the consequences for her with those for himself. Silvia Zsoldos, too, concealed nothing from a student and gave her a second chance. Janice Kemp, possessed of perhaps the most important pedagogical virtue, memory, is flexible with students as a professor once was with her. The judgment seat, she writes, is "uncomfortable," but just as her teacher's willingness to engage in "messy human affairs" had enormous consequences for her, so too she will not take recourse in the ivory tower defense mechanism of ignoring them as a way to avoid fully human responsibility for her students.

These vignettes capture in microcosm the teacher as a professional "in wholeness wholly attending." Socially and politically responsible teachers cannot wait for what will never take place: the consolidation of purposes and standards at every level of the institutions in which they are embedded. They neither slough off on others responsibility for the challenges awaiting them in the classroom nor seek to ignore and insulate themselves from the longer term consequences of their pedagogical decisions. They are actors in the fullest sense in the political dramas of teacher, *taking power* in order to empower their students, so as to prepare them in turn to be politically responsible citizens of their own worlds.

John J. MacAloon is assistant professor in the Social Sciences Collegiate Division of the University of Chicago and member of its Committee on Social Thought. He has been a faculty member of the Aspen Institute of Humanities Studies.

Section 4:

Conclusions

Becoming a good teacher involves combining technical skills with human sensibilities so that both science and art contribute to success.

Conclusions

Warren Bryan Martin

As it is easier to become a parent than it is to be a good parent, so it is easier — however difficult— to become a teacher than it is to be a good teacher. The good teacher, like the good parent, combines technical skills with human sensibilities so that both science and art contribute to success.

In this collection of statements about teaching, we see how often good teaching is a laboratory event and an artistic presentation, how it usually combines the skillful use of technique or "know-how" joined with interpretation, explication, and the pursuit of questions like "so what?"

We see in these reports how intertwined human lives can become when the teacher is available as a person as well as a professional and the learner is available as a person as well as a student. Some of these "moments" are as disquieting as they are informative. A lot of assumptions about human nature, about interrelationships, and about social organizations, bubble to the surface as some of the contributors, in their reports, stir up the murky depths of motivation and meaning.

What else do we learn from an assessment of these moments in teaching and learning? More particularly, what do the statements say about these teachers? As so often happens when any of us reports

W. Martin (Ed.). *New Directions for Teaching and Learning: New Perspectives on Teaching and Learning,* no. 7. San Francisco: Jossey-Bass, September 1981

something that is intended to be primarily about other people, our reports say more about the reporters than about that which is reported or, in this instance, more about these teachers than about teaching.

We know that college is not limited to academic study, any more than it is to cognitive development. The development of the life of the student's mind may properly be the teacher's main concern, but the instructor knows, and these reports emphasize, that the whole person makes the response. The moments contributed by the faculty members show these teachers struggling not only with subject matter and the improvement of the students' basic skills but also with the emotions, will, and other noncognitive dimensions of their highly charged relationships with students. The faculty members strive to maintain balance as they work with students, acknowledging the importance of body and spirit while trying to keep the learner focused on the business of the mind.

The teachers who provide our case studies may not be typical faculty members, but they are not rare oddities either. They represent a large number, perhaps even a still growing number of teachers for whom the traditional, narrow concentration on the training of the mind gives way to concern for the development of the whole person.

Should anything more be said about the contributors to this book? It is evident that most of these teachers sense that today in academe is, as we say, a buyer's market. Colleges and universities live by their ability to enlist and retain students. The faculty members providing these case studies try hard to please students. And when there are difficulties, they question themselves as quickly and persistently as they question the students. The implication is that faculty today are not as rigid and unbending, not as insensitive and self-serving as they are reported to be. The teachers that we have learned to know through the reports of moments in teaching and learning seem capable of change, curious about innovations, quite ready to criticize themselves and join the search for better procedures and more satisfying outcomes.

Furthermore, the adaptability of these faculty members is not merely a consequence of market conditions. The reader of the statements gets the impression that the best college teachers really like their students and will gladly become engaged with those students in the mysteries of teaching and learning. Some of these teachers sound tired but not one of them seems cynical.

Over the last twenty-five years, we have heard that individualism is rampant among faculty and that faculty are capable of collective commitments only with their professional guilds. If that was formerly the case, it is not now. Not among these faculty members. They seem open to collaboration. They yearn for membership in a vital cross-disciplinary, value-centered community. They act as though they feel loyalty toward the institutions with which they are affiliated.

Creativity in teaching, as in other domains, is hard to describe and nearly impossible to explain. Hence, these faculty members often admit their perplexity about why some plan or tactic worked in the classroom. Success seems, according to the reports, spontaneous and almost magical. It comes to the teachers as a surprise, and the reporters wonder aloud whether an equivalent experience can ever be structured or planned into being. But the moments or incidents reported by these teachers seem to reveal that creativity can at least be encouraged. There can be a readying of the supportive context for the nascent moment. Creativity can be taught as well as caught.

According to the theological tradition out of which many of these teachers come, God is to be given all the credit for any accomplishments that attend these mysteries because whatever happens comes by His grace. Meanwhile, however, it pleases God for all of us to work very hard. And these teachers who have dared to write in candor about their teaching—speaking out about their teaching, speaking out about issues and themes that most of us hold in—are obviously hard workers. Their fatigue is earned, but it is made manageable by their dedication to their work and by the satisfactions that they derive from it.

Perhaps the best way to learn to teach these days is not to read the how-to handbooks but, rather, to have teachers describe their teaching—as these professional colleagues have done in the statements collected in this volume. Such descriptions, based on experience and reflection, may be the best instruction available to the newcomer. There are so few opportunities for teachers to observe other teachers teaching, or even to talk with them about teaching, that it is necessary to turn to secondary sources of information. And these reports, coming directly from the teachers, are so vital and relevant that they achieve a primary importance.

What is teaching? For these colleagues in the teaching profession, it is preparation—training, study, reflection. It is also communication—the transmission of knowledge, concepts, skills, attitudes, criticism, and encouragement to the learner. Teaching is, as we learn from these reports, a matter of drawing the student into that special relationship of teacher and learner so that the motivation and energy for the task comes from both participants. In this way, both key figures—teacher and student—find their motivation reinforced, their discipline strengthened, their abilities utilized, to the point that, ultimately, both become teachers and learners.

Teaching is the introduction of new knowledge or, at least, knowledge that comes to the student with the weight of newness. It is also the synthesizing of old and new knowledge, of concept and practice, or other creative blendings where the outcome shows promise of being greater than the sum of the parts.

Teaching is, our fellow teachers report, the application of that which is taught to its point of reference— the individual or society or whatever. It is hard to conclude that these teachers would favor the assertion that teaching is an end in itself.

Teaching is an example of learning at work, even as it is the creation of an environment favorable to learning. And the teacher is an example— of commitment to learning and ideas, of dedication to the pursuit of truth, of the teaching profession with its high standards at work in real settings day by day.

The moments reported in this book are not only passing events, they are memorials to the courage, honesty, and dedication, to the faith, hope, and love of these and many other members of the profession of teaching— a profession that, among its satisfactions, provides for learning through teaching.

Index

Theology, teaching of, 25-26, 39-41
Thompson, E. P., 79

V

Virtue: knowledge as 102; life of, 9-11

W

Welbourne, E., 107-108
Whitehead, A. N., 100
Williams, D., 141-142

Z

Zsoldos, S.T., 123-124, 147